Praise for *Pro...*

This book doesn't shy away from the truth of addiction, ... doesn't shy away from the message of grace and freedom that God has for every one of his children. Danielle and Rob's account of their family's journey through recovery from addiction is full of encouragement and hope. *Prodigal Daughter* is a perfect reflection of the Father-heart of God—unconditionally loving, free of judgment, and always gracious.

> Christine Caine, bestselling author and
> founder of A21 and Propel Women

Almost all families hit challenging times, but many don't know how to recover. Pastor Rob Koke and his daughter, Danielle, have written a powerfully transparent book describing the journey toward healing. If you're looking for hope and freedom for you or someone you love, read this book.

> Craig Groeschel, pastor of Life.Church and author of
> *Soul Detox: Clean Living in a Contaminated World*

I have watched Rob Koke shoulder the heaviness of life with unbendable faith in Jesus. I have known him to be transparent in both life and leadership—a rare and endearing quality that I know blesses any person given the opportunity to have a conversation with or sit under Rob's teaching. The journey that Rob and his daughter, Danielle, so honestly share will undoubtedly impart hope into every reader.

> Brian Houston, global senior pastor, Hillsong Church

When you feel like you've hit rock bottom, when everyone should have given up on you long ago, God always has a different plan. *Prodigal Daughter* is a beautiful story of redemption and the love of a Father who has a future so great that he won't allow you to miss out on it. I've known Pastor Rob Koke for many years now, and I've always admired the faithfulness and love he displays for all around him. His story of his family is a beautiful picture of God's love for us. Anyone who picks up this book will be blessed by *Prodigal Daughter* and the message of grace and redemption that Rob lays out.

> Chris Durso, author of *The Heist: How Grace Robs Us Of Our Shame*

PRODIGAL DAUGHTER

PR⬤DIGAL DAUGHTER

*A Family's Brave Journey through
Addiction and Recovery*

ROB KOKE *and*
DANIELLE KOKE GERMAIN

ZONDERVAN

Prodigal Daughter
Copyright © 2019 by Rob Koke and Danielle Koke Germain

Requests for information should be addressed to:
Zondervan, *3900 Sparks Dr. SE, Grand Rapids, Michigan 49546*

ISBN 978-0-310-35603-5 (softcover)

ISBN 978-0-310-35605-9 (audio)

ISBN 978-0-310-35604-2 (ebook)

Published in association with the literary agency of The Fedd Agency, Post Office Box 341973, Austin, TX 78734.

Cover illustrations: Shutterstock
Interior design: Kait Lamphere

Printed in the United States of America

19 20 21 22 23 24 25 26 27 28 29 /LSC/ 15 14 13 12 11 10 9 8 7 6 5 4 3 2 1

To my amazing husband, Fredelin Germain,
who has supported me through thick and thin.
To my parents, Rob and Laura Koke,
with deepest gratitude for never giving up on me
and always fighting for my freedom.
To my brother Caleb in heaven,
for being the best guardian angel a girl could ever have.
To my brother Luke and his wife, Katy,
for never judging me
and always cheering me on.
To Pastor Cheryl,
for calling out the gold in me.
Last but not least, to all the people,
both friends and extended family,
who have made my recovery journey possible.

Danielle

To my wife, Laura—
we have walked together through the best
and the worst of what life has to offer.
Your deep faith, resilient spirit,
insightful intuition, and unwavering support
were among the most significant contributions
to Danielle's recovery.
Your strength gave us strength to write.
Without you, this story doesn't get told . . .

Rob

Contents

chapter one

Reckless Deception

— *Danielle* —

I stumbled around the living room floor, unable to string words together that made a complete sentence. I said out loud to no one in particular, "Crap! I really have to get home, or my parents are gonna flip out." At least this is what I thought I was saying. What actually came out of my mouth was a slurred mess.

The scene around me started to blur. The shadows of my friends merged together in a vibrant haze. I remember playing some card games. Then some drinking games. Lots of games and *lots* of drinking.

Their voices confused me. First they sounded far away, like listening to someone on the phone with bad reception. But then I blinked hard, and I could hear them loud and clear. My friend was shaking his head at me. "You're not driving," he said. Someone else appeared alongside him, nodding. Her words were more forceful. "Seriously, Danielle, you're not going anywhere."

I was annoyed. First of all, did they know how loud they were, and right in my ear? Second, had they met my parents? *I don't think so.* All I could think about was how much trouble I would be in if I didn't get home. *How come no one understands this?* I tried to straighten up, appear less sloppy . . . major fail. This was hard to do when a slew of vodka shots and salty margaritas was sloshing around in my body.

I wanted to open my mouth and try to defend myself and maybe prove that I was fit to drive. *But that won't work.* I didn't know what I'd end up saying. Truth is, I didn't want to throw a tantrum and ruin everyone's good time. I just wanted to leave. *I have to get home.*

So I nodded and tried my hardest to keep my mouth shut. *Play it cool, D.* I call myself that sometimes. *Don't cause a scene.*

The room blurred. I'm not quite sure what happened next. It's like time froze. For me, at least. I was alone. No one knew where I was. Shoot, I barely even knew.

Then time resumed, although it was still a blur. I heard a loud noise. It was the sound of the door shutting. I jumped a little but then refocused. From the corner of my eye I thought I saw my friends outside on the back porch of the house. Though drunk, I recognized an opportunity. The house was quiet except for the keys jingling in my pocket. My balance was shaky, but I slipped out.

Unnoticed.

Invisible.

Numb.

Everything went black.

I woke up on the floor of my bedroom with my clothes on backwards . . . not a great look. The world moved in slow motion. My head pounded, and my hands trembled. My first thought: *Where's my cell phone?* I slapped my hand around the floor looking for my phone. No luck.

My heart raced as I tried to remember how I got home. But with my scrambled brain I had nothing but bits and pieces. *The party. So much alcohol. Wanting to leave. The keys. Leaving.*

The memories of the night before were few and faint. But I guess the fact that I was home was good news. *Maybe I got lucky.* But then the thought hit me: *Holy fudge nuggets! What about my car?*

I gasped. *I must have driven home! Where did I park? Maybe that's where my phone is.*

In extremely slow movements, I gathered myself off of the floor and tiptoed to the garage. The house was painfully silent, and at that moment I was not the most graceful human on the planet. The wood floors began to creak under the weight of my clumsy steps. I winced, hoping the noises would go unnoticed by my sleeping parents.

I spotted my car parked in the driveway. *Phew! That was a close one.* I didn't really remember driving, so this was a major relief. The open air began to clear my head. Though still buzzing a tad from the alcohol, I couldn't believe I had made it home. Stars glistened above as I took a few calming breaths. Still trying to flounder my way out of the mental haze, I looked at my car again. This time the other side.

My stomach dropped. I gulped hard.

The driver's side was a mangled wreck of twisted metal. I stared at the tire. The rubber was unrecognizable, shredded to pieces. It must have blown out. Fragments of tread stuck out all over the place like bedhead. I'd been driving for miles on nothing but metal.

Rapid-fire questions shot through my mind. *Dang it! I was so close. What on earth happened? What did I hit? What am I going to tell Mom and Dad?*

I had no answers. But I was sure of one thing. As I stared at the wreckage, I knew I had no choice but to lie my way out. My mind racing, I thought of every possible lie I could tell.

I went back inside the house and sat on my bed, my heart beating out of my chest, so freaked out I could barely feel my pounding head. With the alcohol fog still waning, I tried to clear my brain. I needed to finalize a lie—I mean, I needed to make a plan. Once I settled on a story, I started rehearsing the answers to the questions I knew they would ask. Though this was the first time I had to tap dance my way out of wrecking my car after driving drunk, I wasn't new to lying to my parents. At this point, I was essentially a master manipulator.

It was scary how easily the manipulative thoughts entered my mind. It was like instinct at this point. Owning up to my actions wasn't even an option. The lies and manipulation were second nature to me. On my most devious days, I could even convince myself that my lies were true.

Hours passed. I didn't sleep a wink.

When morning broke, I went downstairs. *Crappity crap crap*

crap, this is going to suck! I was nervous, but I hid it well. It was time to put on a show. I didn't want to be too dramatic, but I also didn't want to come across as flippant. It had to be the perfect blend of both; there's a sweet spot, after all. Master manipulator, remember?

"Oh my gosh, guys, you won't believe what happened!"

My dad looked up at me, turkey bacon in hand. My mom stopped whatever she was doing and raised her eyebrows. "What's going on, Danielle?"

Thump-thump-thump raced my heart, threatening to explode.

"I was texting and driving and hit a guardrail. The one by the front of the subdivision. I messed up the driver's side of the car." I tried to look sheepish. "I'm so sorry." At least part of that was true. I really *was* sorry.

Mom shook her head. Dad sighed. He piped up first. "Danielle, you cannot be texting and driving, but I'm glad you're okay."

"I know. I know," I said. "You're right. I'm so sorry. It won't happen again." They hugged me, and it was over. I wasn't in trouble. I got what I wanted. But what you want isn't always what you need.

—— *Rob* ——

When Danielle told me she hit the railing of the subdivision entrance where we live, I believed her. Why wouldn't I? Everyone hits that thing. It seems almost every week, a maintenance crew is repairing it. And the damage from the shredded tire? I chalked that up to teenage ignorance. Danielle probably wasn't aware that if your tire gets blown out, you shouldn't drive on it.

Nothing about her story sounded far-fetched. I made arrangements to have the car fixed. But later that day, compelled by a quiet gnawing in my heart, I pulled her aside. "You promise there was no alcohol or drugs involved?"

Her answer came fast. And she sounded very self-assured. "Yes, Dad, I promise."

"Okay. Good enough." I went about my day.

But there's a reason I asked.

Six weeks prior to Danielle's accident, my wife, Laura, and I sat at the kitchen table sorting through the day's mail. Danielle was a freshman in college, and Laura was taking care of a few things for her. At some point I glanced over at Laura and noticed a surprised look on her face. "Babe, take a look at this," she said, handing me a bank statement.

The statement belonged to Danielle. Each month, I would deposit money in her account to be used for school-related expenses. Scanning the statement, I couldn't believe what I was seeing: $21.99 to this Liquor Mart, $19.75 to that Wine & Spirits. On and on were charges to different alcohol and liquor establishments. There were at least fifteen in that month alone.

My wife and I were shocked. Danielle wasn't even twenty-one. How was this happening? More important, *why* was this happening? Concerned, we immediately called her at college.

"Is there anything you want to tell us?" we asked.

Silence fell. "Uh, no," she finally answered.

"Well, your mother and I never look at your bank statements, but today we decided to look. We saw some things on there—a lot of charges from liquor stores. What's going on, Danielle?"

More quiet. "Uh," she began. "Yeah, well, I guess those charges, uh, are mine." Her voice sounded shaky. A lot of stuttering. She hemmed and hawed about her drinking and then said, "Okay, well, there's probably a bit of a problem. Maybe it's best if I come home. Uh, I think if I leave school now, we can get our money back."

Laura and I were stunned. We never imagined that Danielle would be drinking this young, let alone drink so excessively she would need to come home from college. Even though she was great at lying, to her credit, my daughter had always been forthcoming when confronted with the truth. That day was no exception. She opened up a little about her drinking the more we talked on the phone. Danielle understood she had a problem. We understood she had a problem.

I can't say I was outraged though. Four years ago, when Danielle was fourteen, our family had lost Caleb, our seventeen-year-old son, to a tragic car accident. Our grief was unspeakable. I imagined Danielle coped with the loss by drinking. I got that.

When Laura and I hung up the phone, we just stared at each other. As tears welled up in her eyes, I stepped in close, and we hugged. And then we did what we had done a thousand times—we grabbed hands and prayed. What sobered us was that Danielle herself, not us, had decided she needed to come home. Because of that, we knew she was in a really bad place.

So my wife and I made the decision to get our daughter the help she needed, and the next day I was on a plane to pull her out of college and bring her home. Over the course of the first few days at home, Danielle made some startling confessions. She had not only been drinking but was also using marijuana and Adderall on occasion. In our talks, Danielle wasn't defiant. She wasn't rebellious or defensive. She was honest and willing to get help. To me, at least, that was a positive sign.

After getting a range of feedback from some counselors—one or two of whom suggested the more hardcore approach of going to rehab immediately—Laura and I took the advice of those professionals who thought going to Alcoholics Anonymous (AA), getting a sponsor, and working the Twelve Steps was best. It didn't take long for us to make a plan to get Danielle the help she needed, and we took comfort that we had a map for the road ahead. We were catching the problem early and getting Danielle help right away. She'd be fine and back to her normal self before we knew it.

Looking back, I know I was naive. But at the time, I didn't think my daughter was a candidate for something as serious as inpatient rehab. I didn't think she had been exposed to drugs and alcohol long enough for her to be struggling with *addiction*. Maybe she was being a bit irresponsible, maybe she was developing unhealthy coping mechanisms, but she wasn't an *addict*. The bottom line was we loved her and were willing to support her in getting the help she needed.

— *Danielle* —

I was attending Oral Roberts University at the time, and just like all students at this Christian university, I had to sign an honor code. My signature cemented my promise to represent the school with good character. No lying. No stealing. No plagiarizing. Among other things, I also had to attend regular chapel services, keep my room clean, and not drink or do drugs. I'm pretty sure they created the pledge just for me.

Okay, so I drank at school. Not totally easy to do, by the way, when you're underage and alcohol is prohibited on campus. But hey, lucky for me the guy I drunkenly kissed at my first college party was twenty-one. So I kept him around after that night. It felt like the right thing to do, and his legal drinking age didn't hurt either. As for the marijuana and Adderall, well, that was much easier to find. I didn't have to look as hard because my friends always had it or knew someone who did.

I thought ORU was going to be my fresh start in life. My high school experience wasn't terrible, but I spent a lot of my time smoking weed and focusing on boys, and even then, I knew I wanted something more. Signing the honor code meant something to me initially. In the deepest parts of my heart I wanted my life to reflect these standards. But as soon as the addiction kicked in, things changed.

Honor code, shmonor code.

My mind changed overnight, but I didn't think too much about it. After all, I knew many people who didn't take the honor code seriously. So it wasn't a stretch to adopt that mentality as well, especially when it worked in my favor.

My drinking had some companions. I popped some Adderall in the mornings to pick me up, and then I smoked some weed in the evenings to come back down. Makes sense, right?

Something happened when I drank. It felt like magic. You know that fun alter-ego side of yourself that exists in your imagination? Well, alcohol helped me be her in real life. At first it was an exciting adventure. My friends and I would ditch class and guzzle forties on top of abandoned buildings downtown or go hiking and get high at the end of the trail. I was the life of the party. Always down for a good time.

Drinking brought out my fearlessness and a confidence I didn't have. It gave me permission to be the real me. But the more I drank, the more I wanted to drink. And the more I had, the more I needed. In hindsight, I didn't see this as a formula for addiction but as a prescription to be authentic. I didn't know any other way.

I seriously don't know how I passed the first semester, because I barely attended my classes toward the end. Drinking became my world. But despite all that, I didn't think of myself as an alcoholic. That felt extreme. I thought it was a phase at best. After all, I was in college, and this was what all college kids did, right?

It was about that time that my parents saw the charges on the bank statement and I came back home.

The family counselor I started meeting with strongly advised I complete ninety AA meetings in ninety days. I thought it was pointless. I didn't have a problem. I mean, technically speaking, if I was a textbook alcoholic or even had strong alcoholic tendencies, wouldn't he have suggested rehab or at least an outpatient program?

I didn't think I had a real problem. At least nothing as serious as other people. I was a normal girl who partied a little too hard. I wasn't an idiot. I knew alcohol affected me differently than my peers, but I chalked up my drinking problem to laziness and lack of motivation, not addiction.

I didn't see drinking as a formula for addiction but as a prescription to be authentic.

Sitting through an hour-long meeting every day for three months didn't seem like intensive treatment. Then again, committing to an hour-long meeting every day for three months wasn't a vacation. *Whatever. I will play along.*

AA was interesting. Looking back, I should have researched my meeting options better. As the youngest of my group, I didn't feel the camaraderie I imagined recovery groups would have. I had a very shallow understanding of recovery groups—derived from movies. I thought AA meant sitting in a circle, hearing inspiration, and being moved to tears—that definitely did not happen, by the way. But in the group's defense, I wasn't really looking to belong. After all, I was certain I wasn't like them. *They* all had a problem; I was just making some dumb choices.

I listened to recovering alcoholics, men and women twenty to thirty years older than me, share their tales. Some had multiple DWIs. One had been to jail. One had been court-ordered to attend AA meetings. For many of these people, drinking had led to divorces or being shut out from their loved ones. Their stories were intense, but I couldn't help feeling indignant about having to sit through the meetings. After all, I couldn't relate to any of these people. That wasn't my life, and drinking hadn't knocked my world off its hinges like it had for these people.

Turns out, it just hadn't happened *yet*.

In retrospect, having older people around me could have been a good thing if I had been open to it. I could have learned from their experiences. I could have dived into their stories more. I could have even looked beyond their stories and seen myself in them. But at the time, I didn't. And the meetings started to seem like an utter waste of my time.

Sure, I had been so drunk a few times I had blacked out. And yes, I spent my allowance at school on alcohol. But I never injured anyone. I didn't end up in jail. No one stopped hanging out with me because of my drinking. For the most part, my life was intact. With this backward thinking, I was convinced I didn't have a problem.

I can't remember how many days of AA meetings I accumulated before I started slacking. Maybe close to thirty. What matters is that I started ditching them. And instead of attending, I'd reconnect with old friends living nearby and get high. Then I'd wait until I could act semi-normal and head home. If I was running late, I'd blame it on deep connections developing in my group.

It was during this time that I drove home drunk and wrecked my car.

Okay, pause officially over. Let's get back to Dad's question the day after I had the accident.

"You promise there was no alcohol involved?"

I stared him square in the eyes and did what I did best—lie.

"Yes, Dad. Absolutely no alcohol involved." Guilt washed over me. "I mean, come on. I came home from school to be sober. Do you really think I would drink and drive?" Man, I was a good liar.

Dad touched my face. "I believe you. I really do. But can you blame me for asking?"

I shrugged.

I was good at hiding. Good at pretending. Good at apologizing. A master manipulator, I was good at a lot of things that helped me hide the truth. But I was bad at being myself, and I was certainly bad at facing that truth I worked so hard to hide. A thought began to tickle the back of my mind. *Maybe I do have a problem.*

If you're anything like me, you may be able to relate to the infinite levels of deception. The pretending is so deeply interwoven into the facade you've built that the mask you've been wearing starts to feel like your actual face. The two become one, and they feel impossible to separate.

A week or two later, guilt began to consume me. I needed to talk to someone about the accident. I needed to purge my lie. I needed to tell the truth. The friend I confided in gave me an ultimatum. At the time, it felt cruel. In hindsight, it was a blessing. "Tell your parents, or I will," she said.

Talk about a good friend. I mean, really, a good friend. She was a truth-teller. She told me what I *needed* to hear, not what I wanted to hear. She was willing to risk keeping the peace for my well-being.

I decided to tell my mom first. She's nicer. *Sorry, Dad.*

I was nervous. I was good at getting myself *out of* trouble, not *into* it. I asked my friend to accompany me because I needed all the support I could get.

Walking into Mom's office at church, my palms started to sweat. On the one hand, I was relieved to rid myself of suffocating guilt. On the other hand, I had no idea how to even start the conversation, and no idea how she would react.

She was with someone when I walked in with my support system trailing behind. "Can I talk to you alone for a minute? It's important," I blurted.

"Of course, my girl," she said, noticing the urgency in my voice. She nodded to whomever was with her, and that person left without saying a word. I shut the door and plopped down on the purple couch across from her. Mom, curious, leaned in toward me from behind her big pine desk.

"What's going on, Danielle?"

"Uh, I need to tell you something." My heart raced as I took a deep breath. "I . . . I need to tell you I was drinking that night I crashed my car," I stammered.

Mom was calm and collected. She nodded slowly. "I had a gut feeling you had been." Freaking moms and their spot-on intuition. "Well," she said with a sigh, "you know we need to tell your dad."

"Of course."

I felt a weird mix of emotions. While the guilt slowly slithered away, I was burdened by the responsibility of the truth. This new information was going to change everything.

When Dad walked into the office from down the hall, my friend had left. And then there were three. *Relax, D. Go to your happy place. Deep breath and . . .*

"Dad, I need to tell you the truth. When I wrecked the car, I had been drinking."

I noticed Dad's jaw clench as I admitted the truth. He was definitely not as calm as Mom had been. I could tell he was fuming, but he tried to choose his words very carefully.

"What were you thinking?" he finally said. But it wasn't a question I got to answer. Before I could open my mouth, Dad walked out of the room. *Ouch!* The "leave and walk away" move always stings.

——— *Rob* ———

Of course I was upset. When Danielle told me she wrecked her car drinking and driving, my stomach twisted in a knot. After my wife and I lost our son in a car accident, the last thing we ever expected to deal with was one of our kids being careless enough to drink and drive. I felt so many emotions in that office as I listened to Danielle finally offer the truth. I was angry, mostly at what could have happened. She could have hurt herself or been killed. She could have hurt or killed someone else. She had been driving drunk down the exact same road Caleb had been killed on, and the thought of losing another child on that road to a preventable accident filled me with anger.

God, you've got to be freaking kidding me! I thought. So I walked away to calm myself down and gain some perspective. I had to collect my thoughts and process what Danielle had said. I didn't want to say anything I was going to regret.

Never in a million years did I envision this family dynamic. As a pastor, I would have never dreamed that this challenge would come so close to home. I mean, I taught my kids the difference between right and wrong. They went to church. They went to good schools. My wife and I spent quality time with them. We invested in them in so many ways. Danielle had every advantage available to make wise choices and live well. On paper, we'd done everything right—*so why was this happening?*

I felt an overwhelming sense of helplessness. Everything Laura and I had done up to that point obviously hadn't worked. And now I couldn't reconcile Danielle's reckless deception with her seeming compliance and willingness to change.

I can't remember everything I said when I calmed down enough to reenter the room. But I do remember that I knew I needed to communicate love. We hugged. We talked. We cried. We prayed. Danielle and I have always had a special bond. Still, I was consumed by a gut-wrenching sadness. I couldn't believe my daughter would intentionally put her own life, and others' lives, at risk, especially after the loss of her brother.

What was she thinking?

Why wasn't she thinking?

How could this happen to us?

What did I miss?

My heart is breaking. . .

Later, after having more time to process the situation, I began to realize Danielle had a *real* drinking problem. From drinking at a dry campus to drinking and driving, she wasn't just a normal partying college student. This had happened even with her attending AA meetings for thirty days straight. Clearly something was terribly wrong. Something I was too blind to see the full reality of when we first brought her home. But now knowing the full story, I felt at a loss about what to do next. *What was the right path for us to take?*

— *Danielle* —

Later that night when I was thinking about the mess I'd made, it hit me. I had been driving drunk on the same road where my brother, Caleb, had been killed only four years before. He had fallen asleep at the wheel of the car he was driving and crashed. This realization pierced my heart. My eyes swelled with tears. I couldn't believe I almost recreated that same tragedy for my family.

What's wrong with me? Maybe I have a problem.

Back to the counselor I went. He recommended I reboot the "ninety meetings in ninety days" process.

This time, I gave it a more honest shot. I came clean in my group about the accident and felt a lot of support. For about two months, I went to every meeting. I started journaling every day.

I had a sponsor. I even started attending Celebrate Recovery at another church. Things were going well. Really well.

And then something shifted on the inside. I don't remember the exact moment it happened, but sometime after about sixty days of meetings, I started questioning the truth of my addiction. My mind began to wander. I entertained the idea that while alcohol could be a problem, smoking weed and popping Adderall were probably okay—occasionally only, of course. *Addict* was such a strong word after all. I wasn't feeling desperate for a drink or sneaking booze from my bedroom closet. I felt good, and I thought I was done with the out-of-control party life. I was ready to graduate from recovery.

Not long after that, the lies began to take shape again. I took another step backward. After sitting in on about eight weeks of AA meetings, hearing the same slogans, seeing the same people, learning the same lessons about responsibility and making amends, listening to the same drunk tales of lives ruined, abandonment, and stupid decisions, I started tuning it all out. *Blah blah blah blah blah.* Something about the gravity of being around what I thought were *real* alcoholics made my so-called addiction seem small. A drop in the alcoholic ocean. In other words, I really *didn't* have a problem. At least not now. I had gotten better. I had figured this thing out.

There is something daunting about an official diagnosis. It was too heavy, too extreme. I couldn't accept that quite yet. I was way too young, and I was terrified of being defined as different. I didn't want to be different. I would not identify with being an addict.

So with my manipulation hat back on, I set out to convince my family. I remember bits of the conversation I had with my dad. It happened something like this:

Danielle: "Dad, you know, this AA and recovery stuff has really been helping."

Rob: "I'm glad, Danielle. Really."

Danielle: "And I've been realizing that I was drinking too much at times, but mostly situationally. Not all the time, Dad. I truly believe it was just a phase. A college thing or whatever."

Rob: "You could be right. But still, as your father, I don't ever want you to drink. But if you do, I'm asking that you don't drink at least until you're twenty-one."

Danielle: "Okay, sounds like a plan."

In that moment, in what seemed like a casual conversation between father and daughter, I decided I was going to drink again. Soon. With addicts you give us an inch and we take a mile. Meaning the moment something becomes available or we get the green light, it's all we can think about. I could promise I wouldn't drink until I was twenty-one, and I could have actually intended to keep that promise. But knowing that drinking would be allowed again at some point proved way too tempting. So although I didn't know how and I didn't know when, I did know I would drink again very soon.

A few weeks after my conversation with my dad, I found myself stumbling around the deck of a cruise ship on our family vacation. I was drunk. Surprise, surprise. As soon as I made the decision to drink again, I was like a vampire searching for blood. I needed it. One "harmless" drink at a club turned into a machine-gun succession of shots paid for by "friends" I had just met. Music blared as neon lights shot across the dance floor in every direction. I remember exactly how I felt after the first sip of alcohol ran down my throat. It was euphoric. It felt like reuniting with an old friend. Ignoring my obsession, I convinced myself it was a normal reaction to drinking. Like something any nineteen-year-old would do on a family vacation cruise.

What wasn't normal was what happened a few hours later. After having a great time with strangers, I found myself in some room with a guy from the club. *He was supposed to help me find my brother, Luke. How did we get here?* He was trying to get in my pants. He was relentless. Even after I had thrown up in his bathroom. Even after I had said no over and over and over. Even after I kept trying to pull my pants up while he was trying just as hard to pull them down.

I had enough sense in my drunken stupor to try to get up and leave. But where would I go? I had no idea where my cabin was, but I had to try to find it. Though he forcefully attempted to get me to stay, by God's grace I made it out. The walls around me spun as I stumbled my way through the ship. As I walked down long, quiet corridors, my sight blurred. All of a sudden, I realized I didn't have my pants on. I was humiliated and utterly ashamed, but I marched onward, one wobbly foot in front of the other, with nowhere to go. *Please, I just need to get to my cabin. Someone, anyone, help!*

I somehow made it into the dining area, sat down, and started munching on pizza. By myself. Drunk. In my under-wear. A kind stranger was thoughtful enough to take me to the security office, and someone from security took me back to my parents' room.

Rob

When I saw Danielle, I couldn't believe my eyes. When she told me what had happened, my heart broke. Drinking aside, I was grateful she was alive and hadn't been raped or worse. *Can it get any worse? How much trouble is my daughter in?* As Danielle sobbed in my arms, all that mattered in that moment was that she was safe.

Prior to this trip, my wife and I had pretty much decided Danielle should go back to school in the fall. Now it seemed there was no way that could happen. How messed up was our little girl? The "ninety meetings in ninety days" strategy didn't seem to be working. Was she making any progress? Were we living in denial? Was there any way we could really know for sure what the right course of action was? Laura and I had graduated from the very university Danielle was planning to return to, and we had been so blessed by the experience. We had met the best friends of our lives while attending there, and we couldn't help but wonder if a significant part of her healing would come from her being in the right atmosphere. *God, give us guidance.*

Over the next two months, I watched Danielle closely, my mind a raging battlefield. On one side there were grave thoughts. I would picture her on the boat completely drunk, with no ability to care for herself, and I would ponder how dark our circumstances really were. I would replay conversations with people who were convinced that Danielle was in a much more dangerous place than Laura and I were willing to accept.

How messed up was our little girl? How could we know for sure what the right course of action was?

But on the other side, there were positive signs. I noticed a change. She was different. Better. I guess a big part of me didn't want to accept the "alcoholic" label. That seemed too much, too soon. I just couldn't accept that it was her reality. What would that mean for her future? What would friends and family think of her? Would she be "branded" in a way that would limit her future or reinforce thought patterns that would make it even harder for her to change? And I would be lying if I didn't worry about how it reflected on us as parents. How would we look as parents, as pastors, if our daughter was an alcoholic? I was riddled enough with feelings of guilt that I had failed my daughter, and I couldn't imagine how much worse it would be if people were aware of how serious Danielle's problem was. It was a nightmare.

As the weeks turned into months, we were seeing progress, mainly in the form of her sticking with the meetings, working the steps, and showing an overall positive attitude. It made me feel like we had our "old" Danielle back again. It convinced me that her drinking really was situational—some college experimentation mixed with dealing with the loss of Caleb. I felt sure that Danielle was not an alcoholic. That label didn't seem to fit. Or maybe I just didn't want it to fit. What I saw was a young woman finally getting the help she needed.

School in the fall was a huge decision. Laura and I sought additional counsel from trusted experts. We weighed the pros and cons. We were grateful that Danielle's youth pastors had taken over a church in that town, and Danielle was excited about being actively involved. So after much thought, much prayer, and much advice, we decided the plan to return to college should remain.

"You can go back to school," we finally told her. "But we're setting some serious boundaries in place."

"Anything you want, Dad."

"You're not having your car. You're not getting money in your bank account. You're going to regular AA meetings, and you're getting a sponsor. You have to go to church. And you have to keep working the steps and make wise choices."

Danielle agreed to everything.

I exhaled a bit. Things were progressing. Maybe we were over the hump.

But in matters like this, real change doesn't happen until you hit rock bottom.

chapter two

Hitting Rock Bottom

— *Danielle* —

I could barely sit still. My mind was racing with joy and expectancy. The windows were down, and the music was loud. My brother Luke and I laughed as we sang Whitney Houston songs at the top of our lungs. The wind was strong against my hand. *It's a new day.* I could smell the inspiration and anticipation in the atmosphere—*or maybe that's the Taco Bell I just ate, not really sure.* Nonetheless, I was impatiently awaiting my new chapter to begin. I think I checked my GPS about eight hundred times, like that was somehow going to get me there faster—it didn't. I couldn't wait to see my friends! I felt so good. I felt strong. I felt like I had overcome. I just knew it was going to be different this time. It was a new year, a fresh start, a total redo. So I ignored the fleeting thoughts that tried to remind me of my past. *Future thinking only.*

Finally, after what felt like 4.5 billion hours, we arrived on campus. My parents settled me in and said their good-byes.

And then I was alone.

Wow, they really are gone. I felt an odd mix of emotions. Part of me felt relieved, like I was free again after months of being on a short leash. Yet at the same time I was petrified of this overwhelming sense of responsibility I wasn't quite sure I could handle yet. Truthfully, I was terrified to be on my own. I wanted to be free, but I didn't really trust myself quite yet. If I was mature and humble, I would have asked for more help. I would have realized I was entering dangerous territory. But my pride, combined with my natural stubborn nature, made it impossible to ask for help.

But I promised them I would try. I promised them a lot of things. And I meant them, really I did. I was 8,000 percent sure this time would be different. I even got a little cocky about it. I hiked around campus with a pep in my step, head held high, and the soundtrack of "Eye of the Tiger" playing in the background. Yes, my brain has a built-in MP3 player. Don't judge.

Maybe this time it will really work.

That confidence faded quickly. As I walked around campus, memories returned. It was uncomfortable being back in the place where my life had crumbled to pieces. I was a little disappointed that everything looked the same. I guess I wanted things to look different because I felt like *I* was different. But it wasn't, so maybe I wasn't. I stuffed those fears down, and I told myself there was too much to lose. *Keep your eye on the prize.*

Later that night, one of my best friends from the year before showed up. Knowing there was much to catch up on, we decided to go off campus and grab some coffee. I couldn't wait to tell her about Danielle 2.0.

The familiar smell of strong coffee beans surrounded us as we sat down to talk. We reminisced and brought each other up-to-date on our lives. We talked about the summer, new classes we were taking, and any and all boy updates. Let's be honest, we spent most of our time on the boy updates. We were nineteen-year-old girls, after all.

The conversation was delightful. But as she continued to talk, her voice started to blur because my thoughts became much louder than her voice. I was trying to find the right moment to tell her about all of my changes, but my lips seemed to be glued shut. Then there was a pause. My turn to talk. I hesitated. Then just as I opened my mouth to speak, she spoke first, blurting out this one average, terrifying, exciting, and fateful sentence: "I can't wait to party with you this year."

Uh-oh!

My stomach dropped. Then followed an avalanche of thoughts. I ciphered through a million pros and cons in thirty seconds. The truth is, that sentence captured me. My tongue was salivating. The memories came flooding back, and the funny thing was, only the good memories seemed to return. I conveniently failed to remember all the bad parts about drinking. In that single moment I forgot everything I had been fighting for—everything I was *still* fighting for.

It is fascinating how my brain has the ability to convince myself of anything I want badly enough. In a split second,

I went from being completely devoted to bettering my life and changing my behavior to being completely convinced that any change was unnecessary. Painting a pretty picture for myself, however unreal it may be, is like breathing air to me.

Time moved in slow motion. It felt like I took forever to consider my options, but the reality is all it took was thirty seconds. Yep, thirty freaking seconds.

My response sealed my fate: "Let's do it." Three huge, small words.

That was the beginning of the end. That night, I drank.

Rob

We dropped Danielle off at school for a second time.

I looked around the campus, and a flood of memories returned. I met my wife there. I remembered the first time I saw her. She was the most beautiful woman I had ever laid eyes on. And she was smart too. She was doing her pre-med, having graduated early from high school and having tested out of a year of college.

I like to say I won the marriage jackpot with my wife. Laura graduated at the top of her class and can run mental circles around me any day. Meanwhile, I graduated in the part of the class that made the upper half possible. She is also kind, compassionate, insightful, full of faith, energetic—and she lives life with joy and laughter. Laura is my soul mate in every way, and I couldn't be more grateful to God for bringing her into my life.

Not only that, but some of Laura's best friends married some of my best friends, and as couples we became friends for life. All of it happened because we met at ORU.

I was hoping for the same wonderful experiences for Danielle on that campus. *This is going to work. This is a positive place where she can really grow. This is a place of faith where her dreams can come true and she can develop lifelong friends . . .*

After unpacking the car and getting her room ready, we got in a little circle, grabbed hands, and prayed.

Danielle began. "Father, thank you for this second chance. Give Mom and Dad peace."

I followed. "Father, give Danielle strength and wisdom in this fresh new start. Surround her with your presence and give her great friends. Give her discernment and courage to make the right choices. Put a hedge of protection around her. Thank you for being the God of new beginnings."

Driving away from campus, I was hopeful, but a cloud of worry still haunted me. Ultimately, you never really know what is going to happen. Life is a risk. There are no guarantees. Think about the risk God took with Adam and Eve when he gave them the ability to choose. I imagine God could have created us differently. He could have preprogrammed us to do the right thing and thereby avoid lots of bad choices and lots of pain and suffering.

But if there was no choice, there would be no love. I suppose we could force our children to say to us, "I love you," but that's not real. They're just words. It's only when they express love on their own, flowing from their own free will, that their love has power and the beauty of authenticity and truth. And that's what God wanted with us above all else—*love*. And at first Adam and Eve chose to love God, and life was beautiful and rich and pure. It was perfect. And then Adam and Eve chose differently.

In my heart, I knew that Danielle could also choose to stray from the path that would lead her to a healthy, happy life. Ultimately, she got to choose, and I couldn't ignore the very real possibility that she could choose to travel down a destructive road. Even worse, I knew that there was only so much I could do to stop her from making those bad choices, because these choices were ones she would have to make on her own.

Sometimes I wish God would've just preprogrammed us . . .

Maybe Laura was picking up on something that I was unaware of because she cried off and on during the eight-hour drive back to Austin. Laura has always been a little bit more intuitive than me and a little bit more realistic. I have the tendency to be more naive, believing the best of people. While this is certainly a positive trait on paper, sometimes my optimism was just me trying really hard not to see the ugly reality. My desire to believe the best of Danielle was often just some misguided attempt to appear like I had my act together. I wondered why I felt the pressure to appear perfect. Maybe it was a pastor thing. Maybe it was a human thing. Or maybe it was just me.

Unpacking my emotions was not an easy thing to do. At times I was really scared as I thought about what her life looked like now that she was on her own again in college. I felt like we were battling some hidden force that we were completely unprepared for. At times I wondered if I was overreacting, but some days I felt overwhelming sadness. We had one daughter, and it felt like the innocence was lost. Sometimes I felt jittery. Like I was waiting for the other shoe to drop. On those days every phone call would trigger a stab to the gut. *What bad thing was coming next?*

Of course, some days we were really hopeful. We both felt that Danielle was in a good place, but I could tell that I was a little bit more "hopeful" and Laura was a little bit more "concerned." Whoever said "parenting isn't for cowards" knew what they were talking about. Launching your children into their future is not easy under the best of circumstances, and when I thought about our track record with Danielle, there was certainly lots of room for concern. But with Laura's tears and my hope, we tried to trust God with our precious girl.

As Danielle started her fall semester, we fell back into full church mode. The fall is always super busy for us, but Danielle was never far from our thoughts and prayers. We talked multiple times every week. Things seemed to be going well with her, and so we relaxed into our typical demanding routines.

In November, I looked forward to traveling to Uganda on a mission trip. Over the years, I've visited Africa on more than ten different occasions. I love Africa, and I was excited about the chance to return.

Both my church family and my own family had made big investments in Africa, with both our time and our money. After our son Caleb was "relocated to heaven" (that's the phrase we've settled on), we formed the Caleb Foundation, raising hundreds of thousands of dollars to help make life better for people around the world. We built orphanages and a hospital wing in Haiti. We helped provide resources for a baby home in Botswana. We built a "Caleb Club" to help underprivileged children in Poland. But one of the most meaningful ventures for me is the high school we built in Gulu, Uganda, to educate former child soldiers.

Despite my love for Uganda and serving the people there, I boarded the plane with mixed emotions. On the one hand, I looked forward to ministering at one of the most dynamic churches in that nation in addition to seeing for myself the high school we had built in Caleb's honor. On the other hand, Laura and I had just gotten off the phone with Danielle, and even though I couldn't put my finger on it, something just didn't seem right. I wrestled with my thoughts the entire flight. Playing the tape of our phone conversation over and over in my mind, I searched for clues that would reveal the truth about how she was really doing. The tone of our conversation had been pleasant.

"Hey, Pops," she said playfully.

"Hey, sweetheart," I said. "How's school?"

She seemed happy and confident. We talked for a long time about a lot of different things. There were just a few parts of the conversation, however, that made me wonder. She wasn't doing as well in school as she wanted, and she was thinking of leaving to spend time with some pastor friends of ours who were planting a church in Atlanta, Georgia. Everything on the surface seemed okay, but I decided to write an email letter from Uganda just to make sure.

Dearest Danielle,

I woke up this morning thinking about you. I cannot put into words how proud I am of you, how honored I am to be your dad, and how much joy you bring to me. You are real, kind, and loving, and you have an incredible sense of humor and insight into how life really is. I love you!

I'm writing you this email because I'm unsure of what's really going on in your life. It could be that everything is exactly as we talked about on the phone on Monday. All in all, everything seems fine, albeit not perfect. If that is truly what is happening with you, while it is not ideal in all areas, you are doing okay and learning what kind of life you want to live. You are more aware than most people your age of the things that you know you need to work on in order to live successfully and joyfully. You have so much to offer. Not everybody takes the same road to the destiny that God has for them, and I want you to understand that I am completely supportive and genuinely excited for you to follow your path to becoming who God wants you to be.

But here is where I'm a little bit unsure: I'm not sure if everything you're communicating to us is code for a deeper issue. I have had conversations with you in the past that started with the kinds of things you're communicating, but in reality, there were other life-controlling issues driving everything else. I just want to make sure I'm not missing what is truly going on. If there are substance-abuse issues that have resurfaced in your life, we just want to get you the help you need.

When Mom was talking on the phone on Monday about the cyclical nature of addictions, I want you to know that it's really true, and some of them are really hard to break. Part of my concern in this area for you has been the lack of follow-through on your weekly accountability meetings and the development of a sincere relationship with a sponsor. I know that's hard without transportation, but in my view, that was a nonnegotiable commitment that you whole-heartedly agreed to in going back to school. If my concern in this area is completely unwarranted, then please just know you have a dad who is trying to do his best to love his daughter. However, if there are some issues in your life that you haven't communicated with us about, we're here for you no matter what, and your mom and I will do everything in our power to help you. We love you, and we truly only want what's best for you.

Praying . . .

Love,

Dad

—— *Danielle* ——

I was kind of surprised at how quickly I returned to my old ways. I didn't even skip a beat. But there was something unusual this time around. Instead of picking up where I left off, my desires and cravings multiplied overnight. My tolerance grew too. I needed more. The typical dose no longer satisfied. My body no longer responded to what it used to. In the beginning it took ten milligrams of Adderall to do the trick, and now I felt nothing unless it was over thirty.

From that first fateful sip, my entire world came crashing down. I'm not joking when I say I spent close to every moment intoxicated by something—anything, really. I was desperate. As my addiction swooped in, the lies and manipulation trailed close behind. A perfect blend, always working in harmony against me, the real me. *I miss her.* And poof, I was in total oblivion, deep in the mire of my addiction.

I was no longer trying to convince myself I didn't have a problem. I knew I did. It was obvious. I wasn't an idiot. My entire life revolved around my next drink or high. If I wasn't drunk or high, I was thinking about how to get drunk or high. The truth is, I just didn't care anymore. This was my life. At this point, admitting to myself that I was an addict wasn't a powerful confession; rather, it was grounds to give up.

At this point, admitting to myself that I was an addict wasn't a powerful confession; rather, it was grounds to give up.

I was numb, dead inside. I figured whatever happened to me, I deserved it or at the very least earned it. I wasn't suicidal, but I certainly didn't want to be alive. My life felt like a roller coaster that I couldn't get off of. At first that feeling was exciting, thrilling even. I wanted to ride that high over and over again. But eventually it stopped being exciting and faded into an endless loop of disappointment.

My typical routine was to drink alone in my room. Lame, I know. But I had completely passed the so-called exciting phase of my addiction. Before my return to school, I drank to maintain my label as the life of the party. Now I hardly had the desire to leave my room. I was in new territory. I had to cheat the system. I wasn't even twenty-one yet, so I had to get creative if I wanted to get my fix. I manipulated almost everyone I knew.

It was very rare for someone to manage to convince me to leave my room. Yet one night my friends begged me to come out. It was Halloween, so I begrudgingly agreed. We got *so* drunk. Shocker.

I faded in and out of consciousness. I remember dancing, barely. I vaguely recall a boy trying hard to steal a dance, and I know it made me uncomfortable. You see, I knew this guy; I had let him down gracefully quite a few times. But he kept asking. I really can't recall much about that night, but I do remember even in my drunkenness still saying no. I guess he didn't like that.

Then I blacked out. Sound familiar?

The next morning, I woke up, my head pounding. In slow movements I scanned my surroundings and quickly realized the room wasn't mine. Then I noticed something else, something gut-wrenchingly disturbing. I felt someone's hands touching me, and they were touching a spot that violated me to the core. I turned to see who it was, and it was him. *I thought I said no?* I couldn't remember anything about the night before or how I had ended up in his room. In that moment I broke completely.

My history was repeating itself. If I didn't do something soon, I knew this wouldn't be the last time I found myself in a compromising position. That, my friends, was and is my rock bottom.

It was déjà vu. The first time I faced this scenario, it was with a guy I didn't know and would never see again. But this time felt different because I woke up to find myself with someone who had been trying to get with me for a long time. I knew him before that night of crazy partying, and I would see him again. It put my reality in true perspective for me. I didn't blame myself for the things that happened outside of my control, but I knew that things could only get lower. What I mean is that I was already at my lowest point and I had no desire to see what other levels I could stoop to.

Two days later, I received an email that altered my life forever. It was from my dad. It was the sweetest letter on the planet, but his gut feeling that something was wrong was spot-on. He and my mom just wanted to see me better. That's it. What did I do to deserve that? Well, nothing. That's grace. That's unconditional love.

I called and told them everything. We all cried as I unloaded months of heartbreak and bad decisions. I told them I was 100 percent convinced I had a problem and needed help, real help. I needed to come home. Again.

However, this isn't a story about one girl who struggles with addiction; this is a story about humanity. Struggle is inevitable. Humans fall. It's a result of the sin-stained world we live in. The issue isn't *whether* you struggle but rather *what* you struggle with? Codependency is a struggle. Anger is a struggle. Overspending is a struggle. Eating disorders, cutting, helicopter parenting, pride, comparison, pornography, compulsive lying, and, yes, even binge-watching Netflix—they are all struggles! This is your story too.

I didn't mean to get all in your business, but isn't it beautiful that we're all screwed up in our own way? Say it with me: *"We are all screwed up."* I don't know about you, but I find that oddly comforting. It doesn't matter who you are; you are not alone. We all may be screwed up, but we all can accept the wonderful grace that God is extending to us. I saw that grace lived out firsthand in how my parents reacted to me owning up to my addiction. Yes, I hit rock bottom, friends, but let me tell you, it is the best thing that ever happened to me.

——— *Rob* ———

I stared at my computer screen. Danielle had responded to my email. I read the words over and over. "You might want to trust your gut on this one."

Oh, Danielle, my sweet Danielle.

My mind raced with the implications of those words. I felt a flash of anger as I thought about all of our "great" conversations over the past few months, but most of all I felt overwhelmingly sad. I was sitting on my bed in a hotel room on the other side of the world, fighting hopelessness. I picked up the phone and called Laura, and together we came to grips with the fact that our daughter was in desperate trouble. Again.

With the miracle of modern cell phone technology, Danielle, Laura, and I talked, even though we were in three different cities.

"I'm so sorry, Mom and Dad. My life is out of control. I need to come home."

The next half hour was spent in a conversation filled with details we had heard before—only the names and dates had changed. Danielle was using Adderall to get revved up; she was drinking alcohol to relax and calm down; and she was going to lots of parties. However, the thing that stuck out most was not the wild times she was having with friends but the haunting routine of drugs and alcohol she was doing privately in her room while missing out on classes and missing out on life.

We immediately made arrangements for a family friend to drive up to school and bring Danielle home. That very same week, Laura was hosting our annual women's conference with thousands of women coming from all over Texas, and I had a few days left in Africa.

One question seemed to consume my every waking moment: How do people change? More specifically, how could *Danielle* change?

I examined the trajectory of Danielle's life, and it looked like a graph of a horrible stock market season, a heartbreakingly downward trend with a few upticks of sincere "pledges to change" along the way. I've always heard that people change for one of two reasons. On the positive side, people change when they see the benefits of changing. On the negative side, people change when the pain of their current lifestyle choices becomes unbearable. For addicts, change almost always comes from the second option. They call it "hitting rock bottom."

How do you know if you've hit rock bottom? Well, that's an interesting question. It's hard to tell. There are many times when you think you've hit rock bottom only to discover that you were closer to the penthouse than the basement. Depending on the circumstances, the journey can be treacherously long and painful. And it doesn't help much when you're as unaware as I was.

I thought Danielle hit rock bottom when her drinking was first discovered. We brought her home from college, after all. That's a big deal, especially when you live in a fishbowl like we do. Lots of people would find out that something didn't go according to plan.

Then I thought Danielle hit rock bottom when she wrecked the car.

Surely Danielle hit rock bottom when she narrowly avoided rape on the cruise ship. Or so I'd thought.

As I wandered the streets of Kampala, contemplating the repercussions of Danielle coming home from college a second time, I wondered, *Is* this *rock bottom?*

On the journey to recovery we were introduced to the term "relational and professional wreckage." We met people from all different walks of life who were struggling through the same challenges we were. Although it didn't feel like it at the time, we realized the relational and professional wreckage in Danielle's experience was less than that of some of the other families and people we interacted with.

Let me pause for a second and say that it's never helpful to compare your situation to someone else's. On the one hand, if you compare yourself to someone else and you don't think your situation is as bad, you may feel tempted to not seek the help you need. On the other hand, if you compare yourself to someone else and your situation is much worse, you may be tempted to lose hope. Comparisons are seldom helpful. I only mention the stories of others battling addiction to validate the very real pain and heartache that families experience.

We met a husband who endured twenty years of lies and broken promises and was on the verge of financial ruin because of the alcoholic addiction of his wife.

We met a family who was traumatized by the drug addiction of a son and brother that led to huge legal ramifications.

We met another family who was raising the two out-of-wedlock children of a daughter and sister who couldn't stay sober long enough to care for them.

So how do you know if you've hit rock bottom when it can look so different for each person? Here's what I've learned. You reach rock bottom when you know you have lost control of your life. I'm not talking about a vague intuition but a *real knowing* that your life has spun to a place that is utterly unmanageable and nothing like you would ever want for yourself. Rock bottom is something you can't really explain or understand until you're right in the thick of it. And early detection is a huge advantage, just like early detection with cancer dramatically increases the potential for healing. Just like an early warning can help reduce the damage of an incoming hurricane or tornado. Early recognition that your life is out of control will spare you a great deal of relational and professional wreckage. But it's amazing how much denial we are capable of.

I don't have a problem . . .

I can handle it . . .

I can stop anytime I want . . .

I'll change later . . .

In AA's Twelve Steps, the first step to recovery is admitting that you are powerless over alcohol and that your life has become unmanageable. No matter what the addiction is, the healing starts the same way.

You are powerless over alcohol.

You are powerless over drugs.

You are powerless over sexual addictions.

You are powerless over eating disorders.

You are powerless over anger.

You are powerless over . . .

Life has become unmanageable.

Without that admission and understanding, your life will be caught in the endless cycle of pledges to do better and subsequent failure.

As I replayed the conversation I'd had with Danielle, I wondered if she had really come to an end of herself.

While I didn't know about Danielle, I knew *I* had. I didn't know what to do to help her. I was out of ideas and realized I was in way over my head. Everything I could think of seemed shallow and ineffective. This problem was so much bigger than the combined emotional, intellectual, and physical resources I had to handle it. When my imagination really kicked into gear, I started projecting a lifetime of pain and heartache for us and Danielle. My chest tightened at the thought of what could be in my family's future, in my daughter's future.

Lord, I am at the end.

But isn't coming to an end of yourself a good thing? That's what

I've always believed and what I teach as a pastor. Coming to an end of yourself is a good thing for everyone, and not just for those struggling with addiction.

That's how many people come into a relationship with God in the first place. They recognize they are powerless and either have made a mess of their lives or are terrifyingly capable of doing so. They come to grips with the fact that

This problem was so much bigger than the combined emotional, intellectual, and physical resources I had to handle it.

they are separated from God and there's nothing they can do about it. They recognize their need for a Savior. And they put their trust in him.

And it doesn't stop there. After we give our hearts to the Lord, we realize we all have issues we have to deal with. Some are smaller issues with limited impact. Others are huge and life-controlling, but we all have issues. If you don't think you have issues, then *that* is your issue, because we all struggle with stuff. Welcome to the human race. In fact, one of the greatest leaders in the history of Christianity, the apostle Paul, understood what it was like to struggle with himself:

> What I don't understand about myself is that I decide one way, but then I act another, doing things I absolutely despise. . . . I obviously need help! I realize that I don't have what it takes. I can will it, but I can't do it. I decide to do good, but I don't really do it; I decide not to do bad, but then I do it anyway. My decisions, such as they are, don't result in actions. Something has gone wrong deep within me and

gets the better of me every time . . . I've tried everything and nothing helps. I'm at the end of my rope. Is there no one who can do anything for me?

Romans 7:15–20, 24 MSG

What is Paul saying?

I do the things that aren't good for me.

I do them even when I know they are self-destructive.

I do them even when I know in my heart that I don't want to.

And I don't do the things that are good for me.

Not being able to control yourself is not just an addict's problem; it is a *human* problem. Granted, not everyone faces the same relational and professional wreckage. Not every behavior incurs the same consequences. But everyone has issues. And everyone needs a Savior. And everyone must come to the end of themselves and recognize that they need help.

The truth is that Danielle was not the only one in this story who needed to hit rock bottom. I did too. As a parent *I had to come to an end of myself.*

I took off my pastor's Superman cape.

I folded up my Superdad T-shirt.

And I embraced the reality that there was so little that I really controlled.

As soon as the apostle Paul admitted his life was out of control, he threw out this question: "Is there no one who can do anything for me?" (Romans 7:24 MSG). And then he answered the question: "The answer, thank God, is that Jesus Christ can and does" (Romans 7:25 MSG).

chapter three

Going All In

— *Danielle* —

The hardest part was over, and the truth was in the air. *No turning back.* The emotions I felt were complex. I simultaneously felt the weight of my bad decisions combined with the relief of making them known. This made my stomach hurt, but in a good way, I think.

During this time, my mom was in the middle of her annual women's conference and my dad was in Africa, so they sent Barb to get me. Barb is like a second mom. I'd even venture to say she helped raise me. She has been assisting our family since I was six months old. She loves our family. She *is* family. Needless to say, it was not a hard decision for her to come. She dropped everything and was on her way.

Next up, I had to tell my friends. I was not excited about that. Fear filled me, but not because of what they would think.

I knew I'd have their support. I mean, it was rather obvious that I had a problem. Instead, I was scared because a huge part of me didn't want to say good-bye.

You see, for me, saying good-bye to my friends represented something deeper. People weren't my only companions. Indeed, I had built quite the bond with Mr. Jack Daniels and Mrs. Adderall. If I am being really honest, I'd say my relationship with alcohol and drugs went deeper than a friendship. In a weird way, they became soul mates to me. They were always there when I needed them; they knew me; and they embraced me when life didn't. Even if just for a moment, they always made me feel better. When you build that kind of a bond with someone or something, it's not so easy to leave them behind.

The connections I had with most people were shallow. I don't think I had a single friend I hadn't manipulated at some point. So I rationalized that my leaving was better for them. But the truth is, in my screwed-up, weak version of love, I still loved, and leaving my friends was still a loss. These relationships didn't have time to be developed in a healthy way. With me leaving school and all of us living in different states, I knew these friendships weren't strong enough to last, and this was likely a permanent end to our time together.

A few of my friends were sad but relieved I was leaving to get help, and a few of them were heartbroken I had to leave. But it's interesting, looking back now, to realize that most of them have not remained my friends. I could maybe assume the friendships were all fake and my friends never really cared about me, but more likely, I was a shell of a person during that time and didn't give any form of intimate connection a real shot. Or maybe I just wasn't capable of that yet.

I was scared of the future. I was scared of starting over, of finding new friends, and I didn't even know if I would like who I was without alcohol.

Despite my fear, the secret was out. I bit the bullet and told everyone who needed to know that I had a problem and needed to get real help. My last day on campus crept up quickly. So my crazy and ironic friends decided to throw me one last epic party.

The party was at a friend's house. As I walked in, the familiar smell of tomato juice and cheap booze surrounded me. Despite it all, this was my safe place. I know, there's a little bit of irony there. This feeling of safety in the same environment brought me to my knees. Still, the party, the smell of booze, all of it gave me comfort, even as I stood in the ashes of what I thought my life was supposed to look like. Oh, the parallel of comfort and destruction . . . of joy and pain.

Multiple vodka shots were laid out in front of me. All my friends gathered close as we raised our glasses one last time. "To rehab!" we shouted. Sweet, sweet irony.

I attempted for the last time to drink like a normal person. Spoiler alert: I couldn't.

Mixed drink. Shot. Shot. Shot. Drink. Double shot . . . oblivion.

A part of me wished that the morning wouldn't come, but like a cruel joke, there it was, the brightest sun I had ever seen, taunting me.

I sat on the floor of my dorm for hours, just staring at myself in the mirror. I couldn't move. The clock ticked loudly as tears streamed down my face. Why couldn't I be normal? All I ever wanted was a normal life. Work hard in school, make lifelong friends, discover my life's calling, meet a guy—and the rest would be history. That was my parents' story, so why couldn't that be my story?

I was heartbroken and grieving, but I wasn't grieving the life I was leaving behind; I was grieving the life I didn't get a chance to live.

This emotion was uncomfortable. Naturally, I was itching to drink it all away. *Maybe just one sip?* My usual manipulation wheels started churning. *No, stay strong . . .*

Barb was coming for me, and I knew that all I needed to do was get in the car. If I could just wait till she got there and then get in the freaking car, it would all be over. With addicts, it's not enough to think strong; we have to act strong too. So fighting with every fiber of my being, I waited, without drink or drugs, for Barb to arrive, and then I forced myself into her car.

That was the first time I hadn't given into the desire to drink. Believe me, I wanted to drink; the desire burned intensely on the inside of me. Yet for some reason I just didn't. For the first time, I really wanted something different. It's like actually following through on a goal for yourself. Everything in your flesh is fighting it, but somehow, by God's grace, you have the strength in that moment to say no. That's how I knew I might actually be ready to change.

Thus commenced the longest drive of my life. Remember how long it felt on the drive up there? Yeah, well, that paled in comparison to how it felt on the drive home. An entire eight hours dedicated to reflecting on my failures. Joy.

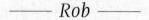

Rob

I flew twenty hours back to Austin with a heavy heart. I knew we were in the fight of our lives. How did my girl get so messed up? I thought back through the years. From the moment Danielle was born, she was golden. She lived with confidence, joy, and reckless abandon. She was the one who would jump from halfway up the stairs, yelling for me to catch her, laughing all the way. She loved to climb trees, play sports, and dance crazy dances. She always had a smile on her face. And she had me wrapped around her little finger. Even the brothers knew if they wanted something from Dad, the best way to get it was through Danielle.

I remembered all the parenting books Laura and I read when Danielle was young. They made parenting sound so predictable. Just follow these simple parenting guidelines, and your kids will turn out great. I wondered where we went wrong and how we could have failed at one of the most important priorities in my life.

I had dreamed a much different dream for my little girl. I dreamed of good friends, graduations, a family of her own, and a destiny that would help make the world a better place. Now all I could think of were the names and faces of people we knew who had gone through similar situations. Some were on the other side of the addiction, walking in recovery and victory. But some were still struggling every day. I wondered how long Danielle's struggle would be. Through the experiences of others, we knew we were in for a huge battle. And I was beginning to realize that victory in this arena wouldn't come without a significant price.

We all met at a restaurant. We were all pretty exhausted. Laura had just finished her women's conference. I had just finished speaking fifteen times in four days and was definitely jet-lagged. And Danielle—she was living on fumes.

When I saw Danielle for the first time, I gave her a big, long hug; kissed her on both cheeks; held her head in my hands; and looked her straight in the eyes. "We are going to get through this together," I said.

It was a foregone conclusion that Danielle was going to require some intensive care. All of our previous attempts to provide support and care had failed miserably. Now we knew that Danielle needed to go to rehab. There were so many different options, and choosing the right place was harder than I anticipated. Thirty-day outpatient? Thirty-day inpatient? Ninety-day inpatient? Close to home or far? Christian-based? A national reputation? There were so many things to consider, and time was of the essence. We had to find a place for her immediately. So even before I flew back from Africa, we put the wheels in motion, talking on the phone every day about everything and praying desperately that God would lead us.

We eventually followed the advice of a trusted counselor, who recommended one of the best inpatient programs in the country, which, fortunately, was only twenty miles from our home. We toured the facility and met some of the caregivers. The campus was out in the country and offered a ninety-day inpatient program. According to the staff, the percentage of people who maintain their recovery after attending a ninety-day program is significantly higher than those who attend thirty-day rehabs.

The whole experience seemed kind of surreal. I flew home from Africa on the same day that Danielle returned from school. The next day, we toured the facility. And the day after that, Danielle checked in. My mind was swirling as the counselor gave us the protocol. Danielle would not need detox, but she would be strip-searched. All of her belongings would be carefully screened. No cell phones or computers. No romantic relationships. Attendance at all sessions was absolutely mandatory. No movies, TV, or music. She was to maintain total abstinence from drugs and alcohol, and her days would be highly scheduled and structured.

One element of rehab I wasn't prepared for was the separation from family. For the first thirty days, there would be absolutely no contact with family, either by phone or in person. And even after thirty days, our phone calls would still be limited to ten minutes. In our entire lives, there had never been more than a few days that we weren't in contact with Danielle either by phone or text. Yes, we could write snail mail, but that seemed a very small consolation.

And to make things even harder, she would not be able to come home for Thanksgiving or Christmas. It was a timing thing.

She was starting her rehab in mid-November and wouldn't be out until February. I pressed them on this point. Surely she could miss one day to be with her family for Christmas! Wouldn't it be healthy for Danielle to feel the love of family? Their response was "no exceptions." It had something to do with potential triggers that could unravel all of their progress. It was hard for me to wrap my mind around the fact that we were saying good-bye to our daughter for a significant period of time when every parental instinct cried out for me to be there for her and support her along the way. And no Thanksgiving . . . no Christmas—that was almost too much.

To top it all off, I had tremendous sticker shock when they told me the price. The rehab program would cost all the money we had saved over the years for Danielle's college education and then some.

Breathe in and out, Rob. God will make a way.

My thoughts were all over the map. I was about to make the biggest investment of my life with my greatest treasure (Danielle) in the balance. Could I really trust these people with her care? Was this the right place for her? It was a huge, super-expensive leap of faith with no guarantees. When I heard that some in the program were in for their second or third time, I was overwhelmed.

God, I need the peace that passes understanding.

At the end of the day, we realized that if we couldn't get Danielle free from this addiction, she wouldn't have a life. It's amazing how a crisis can produce a clarity about what is and isn't important. After lots of prayer and hours of deep conversations about all the pros and cons, Laura and I felt like we needed to trust the process. Rehab had helped many people, and we were hopeful that Danielle would be one of them. And the cost made us realize that rehab was a huge, life-altering commitment.

One of the biggest lessons we learned in the recovery process was this: change doesn't happen unless you make the commitment to go all in.

My daughter's life hung in the balance, and this was one battle I refused to lose.

I was reminded of the importance of going all in when I heard about an acquaintance who had gotten addicted to pain-killers. Over time, the addiction spread to include other drugs and alcohol. He was in and out of rehab, therapy, and the Celebrate Recovery program. After multiple pledges to do better that ended in failure, he ultimately lost his job, his friends, his family, and his reputation—everything. Looking back, he said that nothing changed because he wasn't sincerely committed to his recovery. He was playing games, lying to his friends, family, counselors, sponsors, and even himself. One day he decided, "That's it! I've had enough! I'm ready." The day he went all in was the day his miracle started.

Change doesn't happen unless you make the commitment to go all in.

It's a lot easier to say you're going all in than actually doing it. I was really concerned about this critical part of the recovery process. Danielle started lots of things but often didn't follow through. Was she ready to go all in? Maybe she couldn't.

Maybe the addiction had taken over her ability to make rational decisions.

I wondered if she really wanted to change. Maybe she was just saying she did. She had lied so many times. Was this another one of her stories? Was she just trying to appease us? Maybe she was getting something from her addiction that she didn't want to let go of—emotional or social benefits that outweighed the motivation to change. I remembered a conversation Danielle and I had one time about how alcohol made her feel, how it helped her be more "herself," the person she always wanted to be. Danielle is incredibly funny and quick-witted. But under normal circumstances, you would have to get to know her well before you would see that side of her. With alcohol, her inhibitions were lowered, and she could be the life of the party anytime she wanted to. Maybe that was more important to her than change.

Maybe she won't go all in because she doesn't think she can change. Sometimes I think that about myself. I have been trying to change things about myself my entire life. If I think that way from time to time, then perhaps Danielle battled the same thoughts.

There's an old business axiom that goes something like this: Don't confuse the decision-making process with the problem-solving phase. They don't mix well. First you make the decision, and then you solve the problems. There will always be questions and things you don't know. Most of the time, we don't get the specifics on how it's all going to work out. I shared that concept with Danielle. I didn't want her to hesitate from going all in because she didn't see how it was going to play out. I told her, "If you wait for all the lights to turn green, you'll never go anywhere."

But my biggest concern was guilt. My experience as a pastor taught me that this was one of the most effective tools the enemy has. He whispers things like, "You've already crossed the line"; "There's no hope for you"; "Why even bother trying?" I wondered if these whispers had poisoned Danielle's heart. I wondered if she felt like she messed up too much to ever find redemption. I tried to assure her in every way possible that God's amazing grace provides perfect forgiveness, and that he truly is the God of the second chance. Or third chance. Or fourth.

I prayed that Danielle had come to the end of herself and that she was ready to go all in. One thing I did know: Laura and I were ready. We were desperate. We were determined. That doesn't mean we had all the answers, however. In fact, what we didn't know far outweighed what we did know. But we had resolve and a deep commitment. There was a long journey ahead, with lots of ups and downs to come. But by God's grace, we were all in.

—— *Danielle* ——

My dad flew home straightaway, and we both returned to Austin around the same time. Our family decided to meet at Texas Land & Cattle, one of our favorite steak restaurants. Right away my dad held my head in his hands and looked me in the eyes to say we would get through this. This was uncomfortable; it made every cell in my body squirm. I hated feeling pitied, and I hated physical touch.

When I was a kid, I was an extreme daddy's girl. I jumped in his lap every chance I had. I proudly held his hand in public as if to say, "This is my dad." I was unashamed.

But when I got older, things changed. I cringed if he wanted to hold my hand in public, so I would tell him he could hold my elbow. Shame mixed with the numbing of all my emotions made any form of love, especially from my parents, unbearable for me. Like fingernails on a chalkboard. I couldn't receive it. My heart was closed.

My parents tried to hold it together, but I could see it in their eyes. They were devastated. Sure, they were grateful that I was getting help, but I could sense their thoughts moving a million miles an hour. I think they were confused as to how we got here. Probably going over every parenting decision they ever made, wondering where they went wrong. I looked them in the eyes and said, "You know this has nothing to do with you, right?" They agreed out loud, but I knew it would take a while for them to agree in their hearts.

As I sat in the booth at the restaurant, I just stared at my parents, envying them. Normalcy seemed to come so easy to them. My dad hasn't had an entire drink in his life. He tasted it once, didn't like it, and moved on. My mom was the valedictorian and captain of her cheerleading team, while I hated anything with pep. *Am I adopted?* I just didn't understand.

When they did everything right, why did they get a child who did everything so wrong?

However, I also realized something else as I sat there. I realized that no matter what I did or how uncomfortable their love made me feel, I did indeed have a family who was pulling for me to succeed. I knew I couldn't pursue my recovery just for them, because that never works. But I could do it with them by my side, rooting me on.

When my parents told me they had decided on inpatient rehab, I felt utterly defeated, though my sense of humor remained intact. Thus, my natural response to hearing my official verdict was to break out in the words of an Amy Winehouse song: "Tried to make me go to rehab I said no, no, no." But instead of no, I actually sang yes, yes, yes . . . I knew rehab was what I needed.

The next morning, we drove out to tour my new temporary home. It was in the middle of nowhere. The only signs of life were three cows and many fields of grass with maybe two trees, but that's it. When we got out of the car, the air smelled like straight-up farm life. It was impressive though. The buildings were spacious and clean, yet warm and welcoming.

The staff was nice—very nice, almost too nice. I knew I wasn't being fair to them, but I was pretty irritable my first couple of days without alcohol. Nonetheless, I tried to keep an open mind, even if I was faking it. I would soon be spending three months with these people, after all.

As I soaked it all in, I tried to picture what my life would look like here. I began to wonder if I would make friends or be lonely. If it would be fun or boring. If the food would suck or be delicious.

It was overwhelming. They listed off all the rules I would need to follow for the next ninety days. As I'm sure you all can deduce thus far, I am more of a free spirit. Rules aren't really my thing. A big part of me was scared. I'm not famous for working hard, and this definitely felt like it would require some hard work.

But the longer I was there, the more inspiration set in. I concluded that this could catapult me to a better life—and trust me, anything would be better than what I'd come from.

Embracing this new reality was a tough pill to swallow, but I did it. Because even in the midst of feeling utterly defeated, I sensed a glimmer of hope. I think the hope stemmed from my action. This was the most I had ever done to chase healing. I wasn't forced into changing; I actually wanted it. Hope was and is something worth fighting for.

So I fought.

Trust me, it wasn't an easy thing to do. I had heard all the horror stories. I probably read a million online articles about how rehab doesn't work. Even worse, I soon discovered that 99 percent of the women I met in my rehab house had been there before. It would have been extremely easy to get discouraged, or even worse, not take it seriously.

Recovery isn't something that comes to you; you come to it. In other words, you have to choose it.

But I learned something early on that stuck with me. Recovery isn't something that comes to you; you come to it. In other words, you have to choose it. You can't fix something you don't know is broken. Recovery is a choice; it's *your* choice. And the best rehab program in the world won't help you if you don't admit your problem and make the conscious choice to grab hold of your recovery.

You are not the exception to the rule. You are not a rare case. We all have broken parts that need fixing. The question is, *Are you willing to do whatever it takes to get them fixed?*

That truth set me free. It no longer mattered what statistics said. It no longer mattered what other people did. Every broken person in the world, which is anyone with a beating heart, can choose not to yield. But I had a choice to make. This was my life.

I wanted change.

I needed change.

I was desperate for change.

I was all in.

chapter four

Rehab

—— *Rob* ——

I woke up with a sense that something big was happening. I just couldn't tell if it was going to be good or bad. Not the most optimistic way to start a major investment in the most important healing journey of our lives, but this was one of the biggest leaps of faith we had taken as a family. Danielle was going to rehab.

We packed the things Danielle would need for three months away from home. The rehab center had a very specific list of what you could and could not bring, but at least the dress code wouldn't be a problem, since they allowed sweatpants and T-shirts, Danielle's typical fashion choice. Toiletries, comfortable shoes, pants, shirts, workout stuff, Bible, journal, and photos of her family and friends and her dog, Mellow, all found their way into a single suitcase. Laura made sure she had everything she needed.

I wondered if there was something I should do to make the morning special. But nothing earth-shattering or noteworthy jumped into my head. A big hug and a heartfelt "I love you" would have to do. I was hoping to at least eat breakfast together one final time, but there were too many last-minute details to sort out and not enough time.

The drive over to the rehab center was pretty emotional. We had faith that sending her to rehab was the right choice, but we also had plenty of doubts and questions. Were we doing the right thing? Was this the right place? Why couldn't we just lay hands on her and pray to fix this whole thing? Still, in the midst of the doubt and the questions, we desperately held on to the promises that helped us fight back against the hopelessness. Didn't the Word of God assure us that nothing is impossible if we believed (Matthew 19:26)? Still, I found myself praying the words that long ago, a helpless, grieving parent cried out to Jesus: "I do believe; help me overcome my unbelief!" (Mark 9:24).

For most of the journey to the rehab center, we were all pretty quiet, processing on our own. I looked to my right and saw Laura staring out the window. I looked in the rearview mirror and saw our daughter doing the same. I would give more than just a penny for their thoughts, but somehow silence seemed to match the mood.

As we drove onto the campus, we passed the dorm that housed the men and pulled up to the house for women that would be her new home. We unloaded her things and glanced around at the other women who were already in the program.

We'd been told that the residents in the program were anywhere from age eighteen to fifty, most single and some married. As I looked around, I could see it was a diverse group, from different ethnic backgrounds and stages of life. Some were even mothers. But all of them were there to face their addictions and hopefully find recovery. Danielle would get to know them pretty well, and I couldn't help but wonder if they would be a positive or detrimental influence. Would they be as serious as Danielle about their recovery? Would Danielle be safe? Or would she learn from her fellow residents about drugs she might like to try upon her release?

God, help her!

After she got settled in, we circled up once again to pray and ask God to do what we knew only he could do to heal our little girl. Then we said our good-byes with long hugs.

As we drove off the campus, I struggled with the fact that I would not be able to connect with Danielle and process her journey beside her. Everything in my body screamed that maintaining the rehab's no-contact rule for the first thirty days was a huge mistake. How could separating her from her family be the right choice, especially in those first days of rehab? I realized that maybe for some patients, the family dynamics were so messed up that it would be a good thing for there to be some separation, but that was not us! We had always been there for each other and had always faced our challenges together. I felt like I was being forced to abandon my daughter in the most difficult season of her life.

How in the world can this be helpful?

Instead of hearing about Danielle's progress directly from her, all of our information would come through her counselor in a weekly telephone update. While we were grateful for any information, it still made me feel so far from my little girl. To help bridge the gap, I decided as I was driving home that if she couldn't communicate with me, then I would communicate with her. I made a commitment to write my daughter a letter every single day. I thought, with the first genuine smile that I had in a while, that every single day the mail arrived at her campus, there would be a letter from her dad. And every day I would tell her how much I loved her.

The very next morning I wrote Danielle my first letter.

Dear Danielle,

How are you doing? That was the first thought I had when I woke up this morning. I can only imagine that there must be lots of mixed emotions for you.

Peace . . . that you are taking a major step to really deal with your issues.

Strange . . . being in a completely different place with people you've never met before.

Concern . . . Can I really wake up at 6:30 a.m. every morning? :-)

Hope . . . that I can really make the changes in my life that I need to make.

Regrets . . . about being disconnected from friends and family.

I just wanted you to know how proud I am of you. You

have always been and continue to be so easy to love. Your awareness of the needs and concerns of others, your sense of humor, the joy in life you bring to everyone around you, and your tender vulnerability . . . you draw people to you irresistibly. I'm pretty sure you will be everyone's favorite person in no time. I am so honored to be your dad. Nothing will ever change that.

At dinner last night, Luke, Mom, and I talked about the family program we will be a part of in either month two or three. I'm sure we have just as much to learn as you do, and there's a big part of me that's genuinely looking forward to experiencing that.

Right now it's 6:34 a.m.—if I remember correctly, you had to wake up four minutes ago. I know how much you like to sleep, so you must be thrilled ☺.

I'm praying for you today, Danielle, as I do every day, that you will be so aware of both God's and our love for you.

Dad

—— *Danielle* ——

It was all happening so fast—in a mere three days my entire world had changed. Four days before, I was a college student, and then all of a sudden, I was going to rehab. I could hear my breathing get louder as we drove toward the rehab facility. It felt like I had to try harder and harder to get any actual air into my lungs. *In and out. Breathe, D, breathe!* I think what I was experiencing could be called stress or anxiety. I wasn't sure, though, because in the past I had quickly silenced any negative feelings with a fix. The anxiety spread as I faced the fear of the unknown. I feared the unknown people, the unknown self-discovery, the unknown future—all things I never had to worry about before. I was scared.

I focused on the sound of the tires on the road to soothe me. It sounded smooth, like the soft hum of a fan. It was early in the morning, so the roads were clear. Although I wouldn't have minded a little traffic.

I shifted my attention to my family, and the reality hit me: I really wouldn't get to see them for the next three months. I noticed how sad that realization made me, which was a bit weird. After all, I was used to being away from them at college, but I always knew they were a phone call away. I knew that for the next three months, that wasn't going to be the case. I couldn't see them or call them for the first thirty days, and it was entirely out of my control. It's so much easier to deal with distance from the people you love when you at least have the option to connect with them, even if you don't take the opportunity.

I began to study my family as we drove. I noticed things I'd never seen before. I saw two beauty marks beneath my mother's right eye, one slightly bigger than the other. I noticed that my brother Luke blinks a lot when he is thinking. I discovered my dad scrunches his mouth to the left when he's getting emotional. I wanted to take as many mental pictures as I possibly could to get me through the next three months.

Finally we arrived at my new temporary home. Having already had the tour the day before, I was familiar with the place, but I wasn't expecting what happened next—a full body search. You know when you're going through the security line at the airport and they unnecessarily search you? Well, it was like that only times ten. Suffice it to say it was not my favorite thing, but hey, it's protocol. I guess people try to hide things in weird places. Let's move on.

After that violation of my humanity, I was escorted to the room I would share with my first roommate, Kara. My mom and I unpacked and organized all my things. She is so cute, by the way; she put things in color-coordinating order and genuinely believed it was going to stay that way. It was one of those small but incredibly thoughtful ways that she showed me how much she loved me and wanted me to be okay without her—even if there was no way I could ever maintain an organizational system as complex as hers. I love her.

With my things unpacked and my body thoroughly searched, it was time to say good-bye. But I wasn't yet comfortable dealing with my emotions, so I deflected with humor. I made some joke about them going home and taking a shot for me. Turns out, making a joke about drinking on the first day of rehab was definitely too soon. Bad jokes aside, I hugged them tight and let them go. As the car drove away, I watched until they were no longer in view. Then I walked slowly back toward my new home, a firm resolve growing in my heart. I decided that if this thing was actually going to work, I had to take it seriously.

When I first walked into the house, it was quiet because

the women were in their daily group session. The director had already told me there were ten residents in the house, and I was kind of nervous. My last shot at recovery left me unconvinced of the helpfulness of walking a road to recovery alongside other addicts who seemed much worse off than I was. I didn't connect with the people in AA at all, but I was hopeful this group would be a different story.

So I took a seat on the couch and waited. I thought that was a good first step, considering everything inside me wanted to curl up in a corner somewhere. I heard the door open, and I drew a deep breath. *Here we go!* The women came flooding out. It was exciting for them to have new meat in the mix, so their curious faces surrounded me.

The first woman I met came up to me with a grin on her face. Let's call her Sarah. She was warm and welcoming. With a surprising amount of confidence, she said she had a feeling we were going to become the best of friends. For a brief moment, I relaxed. *Wow, this isn't so bad. The people here are very nice.*

Unfortunately, that feeling was a teensy bit short-lived when she proceeded to inform me of the alien visitation she received in her room last night. I quickly crossed her off of the mental list of potential friends, and as you can imagine, I was a little freaked out. I felt so out of place, and I started to question my choice to come there. This certainly didn't feel like the right place for me. I mean seriously, how could it be? Homegirl was sober, and she was still seeing aliens. I panicked.

But after I met a few more women, none as unique as Sarah, I started to regain my breath. Then a few more. They all seemed at least sane, but I still didn't quite feel like I belonged. I think this was because many of them were much older than me and quite honestly seemed a little crazy. It felt like drugs had done more to them then they had to me. The feeling of being an outsider set a pit in my stomach, and I could feel myself losing hope and questioning if I was in the right place.

But then I met Stacy. She was sitting out in the backyard at a picnic table, talking to her friends. Her calm demeanor was comforting. She was relaxed and laid-back, and she communicated with wit and confidence. She was friendly, but not overwhelmingly friendly. Just the perfect amount. She invited me over to her circle. Then she began to share her journey, and I quickly realized her story was similar to mine—college gone wrong.

As I listened to her story, I saw that she had learned something during her time in rehab. She was excited about the healing she had received and thrilled to begin her future. I wanted what she had. It was like a sudden jolt of encouragement and energy struck my bones. Stacy was there for only two more days, but her presence changed my life.

I could see myself in her.

All it took was one person I could relate with to put it all into perspective for me. Maybe I *did* belong there after all. It's interesting how knowing you belong can change the way you see everything and everyone. Now not only did I feel like I belonged, but I felt like there was an entire future to look forward to.

I was then able to see similarities with the other girls as

well, even with Sarah. You see, a lot of times, addiction can be paired with mental illness, and just because I was lucky enough to not struggle with both didn't actually make me any different from Sarah. After all, we were both sitting on the same couch in the same house for the same reason.

I met most of the girls right away, but there was one girl I didn't meet until later that night. It was right before dinner, and I heard music playing loudly and all the girls laughing at the top of their lungs. The sounds were coming from the living room, so I went out to see what was going on. That's when I met Brittany. She was unashamedly handstand twerking on the wall. I knew right then that that girl was going to be my friend.

Night one came to a close, and I was beat. Turns out recovering from alcohol addiction can make you really tired. My day was busy, and I was surrounded by people. However, when bedtime came and I was alone, my fears returned. Tears streamed down my cheeks as memories of my family and friends back home filled my head. I knew I was doing the right thing, but I was so scared I didn't have what it took to really beat this thing. The desperate desire to be three months down the road filled my soul, and I squirmed at the reality that it was only day one.

Rob

After five days we received our first weekly update from Danielle's counselor. She gave us a really positive review on how Danielle was responding. She shared about how well she was adjusting and how the program was a good fit. She commented that Danielle had good relationships with the other women in the program and that she was, as I knew she would be, liked and respected by everyone. Just hearing how positive the counselor was lifted a huge burden from Laura and me. I was truly grateful.

A few days after the call, I received a letter from Danielle— well, really it was five letters. She had decided to write me back every day, and she saved a week's worth and sent them all at the same time. In one of her letters she wrote about her spiritual journey.

In her therapy sessions, she had heard a lot of talk about deciding who or what her "Higher Power" was. While it wasn't surprising she had heard that, since the program was not Christian-based, I was concerned. This rehab program had a few strong Christian leaders, but there were also lots of doctors and counselors who had other spiritual perspectives. Not only were all of the world religions represented, but there were a few that mixed in New Age philosophy and Eastern mysticism. This new environment would expose Danielle to a whole new group of thoughts and ideas that she had never encountered in her Christian upbringing. I didn't know how Danielle would respond to the competing thoughts and philosophies taught in rehab.

Despite our worries about the spiritual background of the program, we ultimately went with the rehab program we did because we truly believed it was the best for Danielle, and they assured us that Danielle's Christian upbringing would be encouraged and respected. Still, I wondered how that would really play out. I believed that all of the counselors and caregivers were completely sincere in their desire to help, but through Danielle's communication, I sensed that some of them actually had a bias against Christianity. Some of the counselors had a negative experience with church in their past, and they freely shared with Danielle personal stories of judgment, hypocrisy, and legalism and how those experiences made them search for alternatives. I could understand. Sometimes even genuine believers can seriously misinterpret the heart and message of the Bible and end up causing a lot of hurt and damage.

Reading her letters, I came face-to-face with one of my biggest concerns surrounding the rehab's no-contact rule. I knew that just starting this program, she was in an incredibly vulnerable place, and she could be easily persuaded to give up on God or choose another path. I was really concerned that the things she heard in rehab could turn her away from God and the truth we had worked so hard to teach her.

Of course, it wasn't up to me to keep Danielle following Christ, and she quickly showed me not only how strong she was but how faithful God was to her in this season. Danielle told the counselors that the Christianity they were describing was not the Christianity she knew from her own experience. I was surprised and heartened by how convincingly she articulated her own convictions. She seemed to be able to strike the right balance between being open to learn new things that could help her heal and being able to reject ideas that didn't match what she knew to be true. She was fighting for her sobriety and staying true to her faith in the face of pushback, and I was proud of her. I had never heard Danielle express her relationship with God as personally as she was now doing.

Maybe Danielle needed this exact place to rediscover her own relationship with God and make her faith her own. Maybe this was God's plan all along. I had a heartwarming feeling that this was God working in all things for good. We really needed the lift this brought to our hearts. I wanted to fan the flames and send her as much spiritual encouragement as I could, so we exchanged letters all week about her Higher Power.

I wrote to her first and foremost about how much God loved her. I knew that if she held firm to that one simple but profound truth, it would supply all the comfort and strength she would ever need. I told her that our value and worth come from God's unconditional love, and that she doesn't have to do anything to earn it or maintain it. At the core, I wanted her to know that Christianity is all about grace, and that Jesus out of his love for us has paid the price for all of our sins. I challenged her to see herself the way God sees her—worthy of love and valued beyond measure.

I knew that Danielle was at one of the lowest seasons of her life. I couldn't be there to look into her eyes and gauge how she felt or sit with her at the kitchen table to discuss those big things she was processing in rehab, so I wanted my letters to be filled with the love we had for her. But more important, I wanted to make sure she knew beyond a shadow of a doubt how much God loved her—even in the midst of the lies, the addiction, and the chaos that her life had seemingly fallen into.

She was worthy of love and so highly valued. Even though I couldn't be there to tell her in person, I made sure every letter made that very clear. I even encouraged Danielle to read the Bible like it was God's love letter to her. I knew in my heart that the only way she was going to get over the hurts, habits, and hang-ups that were destroying her life was to understand how God felt about her. Psalm 103:13–14 reads, "The LORD is like a father to his children, tender and compassionate to those who fear him. For he knows how weak we are; he remembers we are only dust" (NLT). God may know how frail we can be, but he still cares for us deeply.

Most of all, I wanted her to know she wasn't alone. Psalm 56:8 reads, "You keep track of all my sorrows. You have collected all my tears in your bottle. You have recorded each one in your book" (NLT). God knows all of our heartbreak and hidden sorrows, but it's so hard to sense his presence, especially in the face of pain. For Danielle and for the rest of our family, it was so easy to feel like God had abandoned us, but in writing to her, I helped remind both of us that not only does God know about the challenges we face, but God also deeply cares. He wasn't leaving us alone in this season, and even though it was hard, he was right there beside us.

I have always drawn comfort from this beautiful prayer from the apostle Paul: "I also pray that you will understand the incredible greatness of God's power for us who believe him" (Ephesians 1:19 NLT). It was my prayer for Danielle as well. If we are powerless to control our lives and our issues, then we need power from somewhere to make changes in our lives, and I wanted her to know the incredible greatness of God's power that was right beside her through the entire journey. With Jesus, there was hope for real change for her, and for all of us.

— *Danielle* —

The first few days were painfully crucial. Everything inside me screamed either a desire for a fix or a desire to run, and I thought about it a few times. Some of us girls even hatched an escape plan, but ultimately we chose to do the hardest thing we've ever had to do—we stayed.

There's something you should know about addicts. We are not a patient bunch. It's not that we don't want healing; we just want the healing to come in the form of a bottle so all we have to do is drink it. Honestly, that type of thinking is what got us fighting for sobriety in the first place—the desire to ingest something that comes in a bottle or a pill that suddenly fixes whatever problem we're facing. But for an addict, intimacy and vulnerability make us sick to our stomachs. It's far easier to hide behind and self-medicate with drugs or alcohol than to stare down a disease that begins with a deep heart issue. Staying in a program that gave no immediate results and no 100 percent guarantees of success was honestly one of the hardest things

> *It's far easier to hide behind and self-medicate with drugs or alcohol than to stare down a disease that begins with a deep heart issue.*

I've ever done. It wasn't until I resolved in my heart that I was going to stay that any actual change could begin.

The good news was that they had us on a pretty strict routine, so I didn't have a lot of time to wallow. Our schedule looked like this:

6:00 a.m.—Wake Up

8:00 a.m.—Breakfast

10:00 a.m.—Exercise

12:00 p.m.—Lunch

2:00 p.m.—Art/Meditation

3:30 p.m.—Group Circle

5:30 p.m.—Dinner

7:00 p.m.—AA Meeting

9:00 p.m.—Nightly Inventory

10:00 p.m.—Lights Out

When I first looked over this schedule, I wanted to cry. I hadn't woken up that early in my entire life, but in retrospect, I really appreciated it. The routines distracted me from my cravings because I had very little time to think about them.

It was around day three that I started really doing some internal reflection. The first thing I noticed was how distant I was from God.

I grew up in the church and can honestly say I knew God deeply at one point in time. I didn't feel judged by the church. I wasn't brainwashed or conditioned to shame. For me, the spiritual problem was basic: I had lost touch with an old friend.

Losing that close connection with God put me in a very dangerous position. Disconnecting from the only source that gave me life left me only a path of death to walk on. I was using drugs and alcohol to fill longings, treat pain, and address needs that I should have been taking to Christ.

Now with the drugs and alcohol gone, it was extremely apparent just how far from God I had traveled. This awareness hit me hard. It was like waking up one day and realizing I hadn't eaten for a year. I was craving him.

I felt such an interesting mix of emotions. I remembered the intense spiritual experiences I had as a kid at summer camps and the sweet intimacy I experienced with God before I let the world define me. I wanted that again. I needed that again. *But how?*

So I did the only thing I knew to do, and I wrote my dad.

I never really questioned God's existence or even really entertained the idea of believing in anything other than Christ, so I didn't consider myself confused. However, I was curious how so many people could believe different things. I wondered if people of other religions felt as strongly as I did that their religion is the only way. I wanted my dad to shed some light on what made Christianity different from the others.

There was a wide variety of spirituality represented in my house. From Buddhism to the spirit of the universe, it was all covered, and I learned about it all. It was fascinating to me. I enjoyed hearing about the history, routines, and rituals of various faiths. I even recognized the fruit of their beliefs in their lives. Though it was fascinating, I found them all lacking because they didn't have that personal relationship that Christianity did.

But I didn't condemn them or shake my head. No, I chose to see the good in their beliefs and reconciled in my heart that if I were to have any influence on them, it would be through my actions and my testimony. I had no right to judge them. After all, I was far from God myself.

I wasn't the only person in my house who had grown up in the church, but it seemed I was the only person who had a positive experience with the church. This made it tough for me at times. Almost as soon as I got there, counselors encouraged me to branch out in my faith. It was never direct, but I had a strong feeling that most of the people I came in contact with, including the counselors, had church wounds that were being projected onto me.

It might have been easy to see this as an antagonistic environment for any Christian to be in, but I certainly didn't see it that way. This was the place that my faith became real to me, because I had to finally decide and articulate on my own terms what I believed to be true. The counselors had some truth to what they were saying. You see, my faith had not yet become my own. Somehow, inadvertently, their comments urged me to seek the truth—my truth. So with my dad's suggestion to start in the New Testament, I began to read the Bible.

I'll be honest, it took me a bit to recognize God's voice again, but even on the days when I didn't understand, I kept reading. I learned that when you are obedient and faithful in spending time with God, even when you don't feel it or understand, your spirit still receives it. It just may take a little while for your spirit to catch up to your mind.

I slowly started to feel that connection return. God's words became clear. What once felt like an old book I couldn't relate to now felt like a love letter written directly to me.

As my relationship with God progressed, the intense desire to worship him also grew. I wanted to go to church and unashamedly lift my hands and worship with everything in my heart. I wanted to scream the lyrics to my favorite worship songs at the top of my lungs and not care about anyone else around me. I used to worship like that, and I wanted to feel that fire burning again.

Thankfully, once you'd been in the facility for two weeks, they let you go to church. And with two weeks right around the corner, I counted down the days. Unfortunately, they wouldn't let us go to my parents' church, but we ended up at another great church in the Austin area.

When I stepped into the church and the worship began, my heart filled with excitement. I was so happy, and it felt like returning to something beautiful that I had nearly forgotten. I'll never forget the first song they played. It was one of my favorites, a song called "The Stand" by Hillsong. "So I'll stand with arms high and heart abandoned . . . All I am is yours."

Just imagine, a girl screaming at the top of her lungs the truest words she had ever sung. The fire in me burned brightly that day. It was glorious, and those lyrics stuck with me the rest of my time in rehab.

chapter five

Dealing with Tragedy

—— *Rob* ——

Once Danielle was settled into her life in rehab, our lives resumed a semi-normal routine, but our thoughts and prayers were never far from her.

A few weeks after she left for rehab, we hit our first holiday.

I suppose there's never really a good time of the year for your child to go to rehab, but it feels especially awful over Thanksgiving and Christmas. Thanksgiving has always been such a special celebration for us, with a huge extended family gathering of more than a hundred people. But this year, no one in our house felt like celebrating. With Danielle not able to participate, we decided to have a quiet day at home. We did our best to express gratitude, but to be honest, it felt like another loss. And our family had already had more losses than we could possibly stand.

Our lives were forever changed in the summer of 2009.

The last week in June of that year, our family embarked on a cruise to Alaska. Toward the end of the cruise, our two boys, Luke and Caleb, were on a fishing expedition with me when I got a phone call from my mom in Florida. She told me in a very worried voice that my dad's sailboat had washed up on shore and he wasn't on it. The Coast Guard had been notified, and they were doing an extensive search along the Atlantic Ocean coastline. My heart raced as we prayed together.

About thirty minutes later, my mom called again with the tragic news that my dad's body had been discovered a few miles offshore. Nobody knows for sure what happened. My dad was eighty-two and had been having some health challenges, so we all suspected that maybe he had a heart attack and fell overboard.

Our whole family gathered in Florida to honor and celebrate our amazing dad, and then we returned to Austin with heavy hearts. The night after returning to Austin, our son Caleb fell asleep driving home from a gathering with friends, hit a tree a mile from our house, and was killed. He was seventeen. His loss shattered our lives.

Caleb was an incredible young man with a passion for sports and a tender heart. He was larger than life, wild, and unpredictable. He loved to laugh and was often the center of attention. Losing Caleb left a gaping hole in our lives. It wasn't surprising that his funeral filled our church's five-thousand–seat auditorium.

We lost my father and our son in two different tragic accidents twelve days apart. Over the next few months, I imagine we were some of the most prayed-for people on the planet. We were surrounded by friends and family who flew in from all over the world to show their love and support. We took a sabbatical from our church for a few months to begin the process of putting our broken hearts and world back together again.

You don't get over a tragedy like that. Instead, you try to find a way to absorb it into a new reality, and every day was a struggle. Laura and I often wondered if we would ever feel peace, joy, laughter, or excitement again because all we felt was gut-wrenching pain. Every holiday and every anniversary that had anything to do with Caleb was excruciatingly painful. There was nothing that could be done or said that could make the pain disappear, but we desperately held on to our faith during that time. It was the only hope we had. If there really was a place called heaven that those who put their trust in Jesus go to when they die, then we would see our son again. It was the only thought that gave us hope.

Over time, through the support and prayers of friends and family, we discovered the strength to take steps forward. We put our trust in God and found the grace to live with purpose again. As the years unfolded, we found our stride pastoring our church and pouring energy into starting the Caleb Foundation.

As every parent who has ever lost a child knows, the losses don't stop with the passing of a son or daughter. The losses keep coming. And that was true for us. It was hard not to think about how we lost a future daughter-in-law and future grandkids. We lost future family memories and future accomplishments.

I knew how hard Caleb's loss had been for Laura and me,

and I often wondered if Caleb's loss was a huge trigger to the losses we were now experiencing with Danielle. Danielle and Caleb weren't just brother and sister; they were also really good friends. Most seventeen-year-old boys don't dote on their fourteen-year-old sisters, but Caleb did. Danielle was understandably devastated by Caleb's loss. She would be the first to tell you she never blamed her addiction on Caleb's accident, but undoubtedly she was trying to numb her pain.

But I also struggled with another thought. I couldn't help but worry that Laura and I didn't pay as close attention as we should have to Danielle's grief journey because we were totally consumed with our own. During that season of extreme pain, we often commented on how strong Danielle and Luke were. But I started to wonder if they were being strong for us. *Maybe they weren't dealing with their own pain in healthy ways. And maybe we were too brokenhearted to see it until now.*

— *Danielle* —

I remember the morning I found out about Caleb. I was at a sleepover with my two best friends at the time. We had stayed up pretty late the night before. So I was annoyed when I got woken up at 6:00 a.m.

When I painfully opened my eyes, I was confused to find my dad above me. I wasn't at our house, so this didn't make any sense. My dad told me in a direct voice to just grab my phone and that we would get everything else later. Still half asleep,

I walked into the living room, where I finally got a good look at their faces.

It was a sheer look of devastation. I had never seen anything like it. It was like they were seconds away from losing it. I could tell they were trying to hold it together until we got in the car, but I had no idea why.

My mom couldn't make it; she collapsed on the floor right in front of me with a loud sob. I was worried, but even still, I couldn't in my wildest imagination have guessed the news they had to break.

My mom's lip was quivering, and she gathered all the strength she had left to mutter out the words I will never forget: "There was an accident, and Caleb didn't make it."

Everything stood still. It felt like the end of the world. I wished so badly that this was just a bad dream—a *very* bad dream.

Caleb and I were very close. Unlike a lot of older, teenage brothers, he intentionally carved out time in his day just for me. Caleb came to all of my sports games and many of my practices. He was my best friend, cheering me on and always believing the best about me.

When I was younger, anytime I had a nightmare, he never hesitated to let me sleep in his bed. He was a great brother. He had the uncanny ability to make anybody feel valued and important, and he regularly did that with me.

I love(d) him so dearly.

I was only fourteen when we lost him. Being fourteen, I had learned few, if any, coping skills. Up to that point, I hadn't really experienced much loss. Losing my brother was the hardest thing I had and have ever been through, far worse than the pain of my addiction.

Yet I would never claim that losing Caleb caused my addiction. I wouldn't say that because I don't believe that. I believe that I was born with an addictive gene, a predisposition. However, I do think his death contributed to my desperate need for something to take away my pain.

Being fourteen at the time of Caleb's death, I hadn't yet had access to the big guns (drugs and alcohol), but that didn't stop me from searching for other ways to numb my pain. My first drug was love, and not in that "cute teenage girl" way you see in movies. I loved hard, and I set my standards very low. I used boys to sweep my pain away, caring more about having love than the quality of that love. I clung to anything or anyone that made me feel better, even if just for a moment. I thought it was innocent—that anyone in my situation would do the same. I had no idea that this volatile mind-set would bring me to my knees just a few years later.

—— *Rob* ——

The week after Thanksgiving, Laura and I had our first opportunity to visit with Danielle face-to-face since she had entered rehab. She was waiting at the front door as we drove up, a huge smile on her face. She ran to the car and gave us a big hug. It was so good to see her again, and she looked contented and at peace. Another huge burden was lifted off my shoulders.

Thank you, Jesus!

She took us inside her new home, showed us her room, and introduced us to a few of the staff members and all of the other women going through rehab at the same time she was. We laughed a lot and mostly kept our conversations light, but it seemed to me that she was taking responsibility for her life and dealing with this season seriously. It seemed she was in a good place.

Still, Laura and I took Danielle aside to make sure she was really doing well. With her typical honesty and vulnerability, she assured us she was. One of the big outstanding issues, however, was the concern of her counselors on how she was processing Caleb's loss. I could tell Danielle still had questions about it all. Deep questions, and if I was honest, I did too.

Even though we lost Caleb years ago, I still couldn't help but wonder why God didn't answer my prayers to protect him. Why did I let him stay out late that night? Did I do something wrong? Was it the devil? Was it just chance, or maybe teenage foolishness? Even though lots of lives were being touched through the Caleb Foundation, I questioned the price that set it all in motion. Certainly there could have been other ways to make a difference in the world.

When some people suffer loss, they question the existence of God. I'm not saying I never entertained the thought, but for me, taking God out of the picture only raised more questions. As strange as this may sound, the pain that consumed our hearts also confirmed the reality of God. For me, the pain of our loss confirmed that we had someone of immeasurable worth living with us for seventeen years, someone made by God in the image of God. Still, I couldn't help but struggle with the overwhelming tragedy of it all.

I totally understood the issues Danielle was wrestling with, and I wanted to help her process them in any way I could. Over the next few weeks, we exchanged many letters, working through the issues of loss and pain.

Nothing could have possibly prepared her for the sudden loss of someone she loved so deeply. It was an absolute shock to the core of her being. I told her that her grief journey would be different from everyone else's because she had a unique and different relationship with Caleb. Nobody else was his beloved sister. She had experiences and memories that no one else had. They were a treasure for her alone. Because people process life and relationships differently, her grief journey would be different from anyone else's—even mine. People grieve differently and at different paces, and I wanted her to know that was okay.

When it comes to grieving, no one size fits all. I knew Danielle liked to process alone, but I did encourage her, when it felt appropriate, to reach out to others as well. I was concerned about the tendency we all have to walk down dark thought paths that are not healthy when we spend too much time alone. We all need the perspective of trusted friends and counselors. Grieving often comes with lots of emotions and tears, and her closest friends should have the privilege of sharing those moments with her. Good friends would know that she didn't need someone to try to fix things in those moments; rather, she just needed to be loved and hugged.

One of the hardest things to accept about loss is that

grieving takes time. It's not a quick process, and it takes longer than anyone wants it to. I encouraged her not to get frustrated with herself and to avoid comparing her journey with others' healing journeys. I knew it had to be hard for her to process this pain years after Caleb's loss, and I didn't want her to rush through processing and healing to meet some standard of "appropriate grieving" that she felt she had to meet. I encouraged her to put her trust in God and walk through this season with him. He would bring her through.

— *Danielle* —

It was a unique experience to process the emotions I felt over losing Caleb while in rehab. I agreed with what my dad told me in letters—that everyone grieved differently—but it just felt like it was too late to work through his death. I had numbed my pain for so long, and now that it was all flooding back, it felt like my "grief clock" had expired and my time was up. Even though my brain told me that wasn't true and that processing my grief would take as long as it needed to, I still struggled to let myself fully feel the pain of my brother's death so many years after it occurred.

Thankfully, everyone from my family to the team in the rehab facility encouraged me to dive into these emotions, and that helped me not worry about some imaginary grief timeline that I felt had expired. After all, the pain felt like it had happened just yesterday, even though the memories felt a planet away.

More than anything, I felt distant from my brother. I struggled with knowing that I loved him so much, and yet no matter what I said or did, nothing would change the fact that in this life I wouldn't see him or hear him again.

It felt weird that it had been five years since his passing. It was weird to realize I was older than he was when he died. All of it was weird. All of it hurt, and I hated it.

Just like my dad had encouraged me to do, I had been talking to God, but to be honest, I was angry with him. I was angry at God for letting us lose Caleb, and I was angry at God for all of this pain inside me. In a weird way, it almost felt good to admit it. After all, I knew I wasn't the first person to be angry at God, and I knew he could handle it. I knew that staying in that angry place too long wasn't healthy, but I couldn't help but feel like God was pleased with my honesty. For the first time in a long time, I was owning up to exactly how I felt—the good, the bad, and the ugly—and I wasn't trying to numb or ignore what was really happening in my heart. Instead, I was committed to exploring these emotions.

I decided I was going to start writing Caleb. Just a page a day. I felt like it would help to have an ongoing conversation with him. I missed him dearly and wanted to feel close to him again.

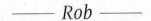

Rob

In one of the letters that Danielle and I exchanged, I shared with her one of the most powerful truths her mom and I learned

as we walked through our own grief journey. It came to us in a letter from a pastor who had also lost a son in a car accident, and he had heard it from someone else who had lost a child in an accident. He told us, "Don't exchange what you do know for what you don't know."

In a season of extreme grief or loss, there's always the temptation to be so overwhelmed with pain that you exchange what you do know for what you don't know. When faced with such a loss, unanswered questions seem to mount every day, and it's easy to let those unknowns overshadow and rob you of truths you had previously held on to. I reminded Danielle that there were some things we would never know this side of heaven, but there were lots of things we do know. We know that God loves us. We know that God forgives us. We know that God sustains us. And we know that heaven is real for those who put their trust in him. We should never let our unanswered questions rob us of what we *do* know.

Still, I told Danielle that I understood how easy it was to feel uncertain in the wake of such a profound loss. A few weeks after Caleb's accident, Laura and I were taking a walk around the block, and she tearfully confessed that God must not be who she thought he was. Either he was "all-loving" or he was "all-powerful," but he couldn't be both. She reasoned that God could be "all-loving" and had wanted to save Caleb, but perhaps he was not "all-powerful" because for some reason he couldn't. Or maybe God was "all-powerful," and he could have saved Caleb, but not "all loving" because he chose not to.

We took a couple more walks around the block as we

processed our hurt. I'll be honest, we didn't come away with any perfect answers, and even as I write this, we still have some unanswered questions. The loss of our son will always be a mystery to us. Still, we didn't want to trade the questions—those things we didn't know—for the things we did.

The cross forever settles that God is all-loving, and creation and the resurrection forever settle that God is all-powerful. So how did this all-powerful, all-loving God let such a tragedy befall our family? For us, we fall back on our everlasting trust in God. We trust God even when we don't understand, and even when we find ourselves facing mountains of hurt and confusion. We trust in God because we believe him to be all-loving and all-powerful, and we have faith in that fact, even when we can't understand the circumstances around us. It's not an easy concept to grasp, and there are days when it's hard to trust. But ultimately, we always find ourselves returning to Christ, and that is what is most important. It's what I wanted Danielle to remember as she processed her grief and worked toward recovery, and it's something I cling to each and every day.

— *Danielle* —

In one of my dad's letters, he said something that really changed the game for me: "Don't exchange what you do know for what you don't know." I let that thought marinate with me. It encouraged me to define what it was that I knew. So I made a list:

I KNOW that heaven is real.

I KNOW that Caleb was saved.

I KNOW that God is good.

I KNOW that Caleb is living his best life.

Those truths brought me comfort. The hardest part was accepting that there are some questions on this side of heaven that will never be answered. The other hard part was realizing that even though I was happy about Caleb's new reality in heaven, I could still be sad that he wasn't here. I missed him, and I will *always* miss him.

My counselors suggested we do a ceremony of sorts. It started with them giving me an opportunity to honor and remember Caleb, but I didn't want all the focus to be on *my* pain alone. I asked the community if anyone wanted to participate for anyone in their life they had lost, and I was shocked at how many people had lost someone they loved.

We all went down to the river, wrote our loved one's name on a rock, and placed it by the river. It was beautiful, and though I had to push through the instinct to ignore my pain because it had been too long, I felt a little closer to healing. Vulnerability was still uncomfortable for me, but I could feel myself slowly allowing myself to acknowledge and deal with my emotions.

I should add that my mom was a huge part of this process too. She also wrote me letters as I went through therapy, and her words had such an impact on my heart. Receiving these heartfelt letters from my parents reminded me that I was not alone on my journey to sobriety and helped me see how important it was to deal with the emotions and pain I had bottled up for so long.

Over the years, I had almost forgotten how to cry because I had become such an expert at numbing my emotions. But as I slowly did the hard work of processing the grief and pain I had shoved into the dark corners of my heart, I began to feel more and more alive every day. I wasn't going to run anymore, and to be honest, I didn't think I even could. And so with the support and wisdom of my parents, I finally felt ready to face the long road to real healing.

—— *Rob* ——

People deal with pain in a wide variety of ways. Some try to bury it; some work to distract themselves from it; and others simply try to diminish their pain. I still wondered if Danielle had done just that after Caleb died. There is a big connection between loss and addiction; many addicts use their addiction to help them deal with (or, more accurately, ignore) a loss or personal tragedy.

Regardless of how Danielle processed pain, I reminded her that God gave all of us the power to choose. We can either run from the grief or face it. For so long, Danielle had been running, but if we run from our grief, we will find it is a relentless pursuer. And when we run, we will try to find ways to medicate the pain. That's where addictions can begin.

It can be scary, but it's far better to deal with grief and pain head-on than to run and find ourselves in a situation where we're being controlled by our relentless desire to escape the pain. I challenged her to be as honest as possible about her loss and suffering. I tried to encourage her that her choice of how to deal with this pain was key to her recovery. She could continue to run from the pain and continue using drugs and alcohol to self-medicate, or she could embrace the pain and learn from it. She could suffocate her life with self-pity, or she could learn to be grateful, even when there seemed to be no reason for it.

If we run from our grief, we will find it is a relentless pursuer.

The good news is that we as believers have a great payoff for doing this hard emotional work. As hard as it sounds, we can grow from walking through pain. Walking through this season of grief and pain, dealing with the loss, and clinging to Christ in the darkest of times ultimately bring greater joy. It seems backward, but I wanted her to know—because I experienced it myself—that God's strength can give a peace no circumstance can shake. Of course, facing her pain wouldn't mean she'd become a superhuman paragon of strength and total emotional health, but she would know God and have the capacity to love others in a way she'd never experienced before.

One of the most profound miracles in the universe, which helps me believe that our God is a good God, is the fact that those whose hearts have been enlarged by suffering have the greatest capacity to love. The apostle Paul knew the heart of our heavenly Father to redeem our suffering. He wrote, "Praise be to the God and Father of our Lord Jesus Christ, the Father of compassion and the God of all comfort, who comforts us in all our troubles, so that we can comfort those in any trouble with the comfort we ourselves receive from God" (2 Corinthians 1:3–4).

I warned Danielle that the choice to face her pain and grief was not an easy one, but it was the only choice that would lead to healing. I wanted her to know that when we allow ourselves to feel the loss, it's God's way of mending our broken hearts.

I shared with her a Scripture passage that has helped me through these seasons of pain and grief: "And now, dear brothers and sisters, we want you to know what will happen to the believers who have died so you will not grieve like people who have no hope. For since we believe that Jesus died and was raised to life again, we also believe that when Jesus returns, God will bring back with him the believers who have died" (1 Thessalonians 4:13–14 NLT).

Grief can feel overwhelming, but as people who believe in God, we do not grieve like people who have no hope. We believe that heaven is real and that we will see our loved ones again.

More than anything, it wasn't just important for me to use my letters to support my daughter and speak truth over her life; I also wanted her to know she wasn't the only one who had done some serious wrestling with God, faith, and her beliefs. It's why I told her about how much her mother and I had struggled over whether God could be a good, loving, powerful God. I wanted Danielle to know that we're human and that these struggles don't mean there's anything wrong with her or her faith in Christ.

Plus, if I was honest, just as Danielle was processing grief in this season while she was in rehab, I too found myself wrestling with a whole new wave of grief as the holidays approached. We love Christmas, and since Laura was born on Christmas Day, we usually celebrate with absolute reckless abandon. Decorations and traditions were firmly established, and our family always loves getting together. But we lost a huge part of that fun, festive spirit when we lost Caleb, and now we would have to celebrate this Christmas without Danielle as well.

Sometimes life just sucks . . .

It was one of the darkest times for me. Not only was I dealing with all the emotions of our family drama, but this also happened to be one of the busiest times of the year in church. With all the special services and year-end volunteer and staff appreciation parties, I was exhausted.

My mind and my heart were racing with questions and frustrations. This was never how I imagined my life unfolding, and I was filled with doubts. Was I going to lose another child? How could all of this happen in a Christian home? Wasn't God supposed to insulate us and protect us from these kinds of situations? Where had I gone wrong? And I was more than just a little bit frustrated that Danielle was twenty minutes away from our house, but she might as well have been on the other side of the world.

More and more frequently, I found myself rereading the letters I wrote to Danielle. Sometimes the most important sermons are the ones you preach to yourself.

chapter six

Family Week

— *Danielle* —

I was becoming more comfortable with my new routine in rehab, but I found I could never totally get used to being away from my family. The separation was even harder for me because I spent every holiday known to mankind away from them during my time in rehab. I missed Thanksgiving, Christmas, my mom's birthday, New Year's Day, Valentine's Day, and Caleb's birthday. I squirmed as I dreamed about what my family was doing to celebrate.

Every fiber of my being was screaming to be back home, but I did my best to accept that this was my current season. I had to enjoy and be fully present right where I was, and wistfully wishing I was back home or anywhere but rehab could seriously hinder my progress.

Addicts often struggle with being present in the moment in

front of them. Whether the present moment is painful, joyful, scary, or exciting, we can't seem to handle it. Over the course of our addiction, we've lost touch with our *gezellig* spirit. *Gezellig* is a Dutch word my family uses when we're feeling the beauty of a present moment.

The truth is, you really only have the moment in front of you. We aren't promised tomorrow or even our next breath, so it's important to be fully present and aware in whatever moment we find ourselves. Once I made that mental shift to embrace my *gezellig* spirit, I was actually able to fully invest in the here and now.

I had to really use my imagination for the first time since I was a kid. There was no "Candy Crush." No Netflix. No social media. Though it was difficult to get used to, it ended up being one of the greatest gifts. With few options to choose from, learning to knit became one of my greatest joys. For Christmas, since I couldn't be with them, I made beanies for my whole family. I thought they were the best-looking, most stylish hats ever created on earth. They were works of art. In my mind, Picasso would have been interested in these hats.

Truth be told, these hats were absolutely hideous, but I had found a way to celebrate the holidays, show my family I loved them, and still be present in this season at rehab. I was learning to find ways to plug into uncomfortable situations and thrive, even if that meant sending my family creative-looking (okay, okay—*ugly*) beanies for Christmas presents.

Going into the new year, I wanted to continue a personal tradition of writing out my resolutions. I have written them out every year as far back as I can remember, but the goals never came to pass. But this time felt different. Now that massive chains weren't holding me back, I felt hopeful that I could actually follow through on my goals. It felt like the most genuine new beginning I had ever experienced.

New Year's Day usually inspires us to think about the whole year that lies ahead, but addicts don't typically do well at focusing on large amounts of time. One of the more popular mottos in the AA movement is "one day at a time"—a motto that exists because it's much easier for us to imagine twenty-four hours without our substance than an entire year. I realized I needed to focus on the day in front of me and work to make that day the best I could. So for my New Year's resolution list, I wrote only one thing: *stay sober.* I knew that had to be my main focus, since the odds weren't entirely in my favor.

To help me stay sober and motivated, I learned as much as I could about my condition. I felt like understanding my illness would change everything for me. I knew that sobriety had to be my top priority in everything I did after rehab. I knew that relapse happens to almost everyone in recovery; it had already happened to me, after all. But if I really didn't want it to happen again, I had to accept the fact that I had a disease that would kill me if I didn't treat it.

Typically for addicts who go into rehab, our initial hope is that we will learn or experience something that will get our drinking or using under control. We don't go into it thinking we've taken our last sip because we want to be normal and consume alcohol just like anyone else. *If we can go to rehab and get our broken parts fixed, we can function just like everyone else, right?* Unfortunately, that's not how it works.

Addicts are wired differently on a chemical level, and understanding why we're different is one of the most powerful tools we have. One casual drink at a business dinner may be a typical outing for many average drinkers. However, for the alcoholic, this casual business drink is met later on that same night with several other drinks to finish the job. One drink isn't just one drink to an addict. For me, I had to accept that even a casual drink activates a huge chain reaction in my body that I never wanted to mess around with again.

In short, being an addict basically means I am allergic to alcohol. If you learned that you had a deadly peanut allergy, you'd stay far away from nuts. It's the same for me and my relationship with alcohol. The only way for me, or any addict, to guarantee a life and long-term health is complete abstinence and living 100 percent alcohol free. It's no easy feat, to be sure, and it's a path that requires more attention and determination than you can possibly imagine. But it's all worth it, because it's a fight for my life.

With all of these lightbulbs turning on for me, I couldn't wait to share them with my family. I knew this information would really help them understand what I was struggling with and how deep this thing goes. I wanted them to see that this disease was not directly correlated to experiences in my life and not a result of a mistake they made. Rather, it is a mind malfunction, a difference in my brain makeup.

The family program was just a few weeks away, and I knew

they were going to learn all about the addict brain. I had been looking forward to this for quite some time for several reasons. Family Week was a landmark for us, a huge milestone. It showed us how far we had come, and with the family program marking our last month in rehab, it showed how close we were to sweet, sweet freedom.

Still, I was a bit apprehensive. You see, the family program isn't just a time when my family gets a window into everything I'm learning about addiction; it's also a time for families to tell you exactly how your actions made them feel. I had seen some of my friends go through the program to have their heart broken, and I just didn't know if I could handle that. I didn't know if my family could handle it either.

My family is very close, especially after losing Caleb. However, I think after experiencing what we considered the worst that life has to offer, we subconsciously decided to focus only on the positive. We were an optimistic bunch, and I never really heard their disappointments, probably because we were a bit too good at ignoring the negative. Even my being in rehab never created a blow-out moment when everyone hated me because I was ruining the family. No, from the very beginning, they told me how proud they were of me for being so courageous to ask for help.

I was learning in therapy that it takes digging deep and discovering your hurts in order to get healing from them, so that would mean staring some ugly, painful realities right in the face, without any rose-colored glasses. It wasn't going to be the time to put a positive spin on everything. Because of that, I had no clue what to expect from Family Week, but I knew that, regardless of how uncomfortable it might make us feel, Family Week would be important to each and every one of us.

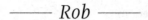

Rob

Danielle had been in rehab for fifty-one days, meaning Family Week was right around the corner. It was a big deal. When we first enrolled Danielle in rehab, the leaders highlighted this as a nonnegotiable commitment. We were told that each day would be filled with information pertinent to Danielle's recovery and that the group interactions we experienced would bring understanding and healing. Family Week included seven to ten other families, so it wasn't just our family drama that would be on display. We would be experiencing lots of drama and lots of different family dynamics.

I had some mixed emotions as I drove onto campus. On the one hand, I would do anything to help our daughter. If taking a week out of my life was important to her recovery, then it certainly was a small price to pay. On the other hand, I could think of a thousand things I'd rather be doing than spending a week talking about our issues in front of people I'd never met. And this may be a surprising thing for a pastor to admit, but I wasn't exactly in the mood to hear about other people's issues either.

To be honest, I was, at some level, embarrassed that as a pastor's family, we were dealing with these kinds of challenges.

My image of a pastor was someone who was spiritually strong, emotionally joyful, and physically healthy—and someone with a great family. I didn't expect pastors to be perfect, but if they had issues, I imagined them to be socially acceptable ones (whatever that is) and not the kind that landed their kids in rehab. Not only was I embarrassed, but I felt guilty and ashamed too. *If I had been a better pastor and father,* I thought, *we wouldn't be here.*

But when Luke, Laura, Danielle, and I found our seats in the large circle, I realized there wasn't one type of family who had to deal with addiction. There were about thirty-five of us in the room, representing people from every walk of life. Every age and stage, rich and poor, educated and uneducated, famous and obscure, could be found in that room. As I heard the stories of the other families, it suddenly hit me: nobody is immune.

Addiction is not a struggle that is restricted to some specific demographic. It can find its way into anyone's life, regardless of socioeconomic, ethnic, or religious boundaries. I soon learned that 11 percent of the American population over the age of twelve is addicted to drugs, alcohol, or both. That represents more than twenty-five million people—equal to the entire population of the state of Texas. You may think your family won't be touched by addiction, but the reality is that more families struggle with addiction than many of us realize.

Throughout the day, we heard lots of stories about the relational wreckage that substance abuse produced. We had our own story, but to hear the stories of other families was truly sobering. For some of the families, this was their second or third try at rehab. We heard stories of families bailing their loved ones out of jail. Dealing with massive legal problems. Rescuing them from prostitution. Rushing them to the hospital with barely a pulse. And so on . . .

We were entering the rehab experience with a much smaller relational-wreckage footprint than we were hearing from the other families. And while a part of that made me grateful, it also scared me to death. If Danielle didn't win this battle, our future would be filled with much more heartache and pain.

But one of the beautiful takeaways of going through a week like this with other families was the realization that we were not alone. As I listened to families tell their stories and express their emotions, I can't tell you how many times I found myself thinking, *That's exactly how I feel!* When one family spoke of the utter hopelessness of not knowing what to do or where to turn, I knew exactly what they were feeling. When one dad talked about his fears, I was all in. One mom was crying uncontrollably as she shared about the pain that gripped her heart. I turned to Laura and saw tears streaming down her cheeks too. When a husband shared with real anger and frustration about the lies and manipulations he experienced from his addicted wife, all of us nodded with a "been there, done that" sense of solidarity. A surprising amount of healing comes from recognizing you are not alone. I felt like I was moving from isolation to community, drawing strength from the simple realization that there were others just like me.

But Family Week wasn't just about finding community with other families going through similar experiences; it was also about working through our family's unique issues. One of the issues that came up was codependency in my relationship with Danielle. I wasn't initially sold on the idea that there was a problem, but it did bring up some interesting talking points for our family.

Codependency is most commonly associated with being emotionally dependent on others. While I often thought that all parents are in one way or another emotionally "dependent" on their children, I wondered if I had issues here. Was I overly sensitive to the behavior of my children because it reflected on me? Maybe this was part of the motivation behind the decision to send Danielle back to school when she was obviously still dealing with major challenges. Maybe I was blind to her real situation because I didn't want to have a daughter with alcohol issues so severe that she couldn't go back to school.

But the biggest symptom of my codependency was my tendency to enable my children by trying to fix their problems and rescue them from the consequences of their actions. During Family Week, we attended a whole session on enabling, and I felt like they were reading my mail.

We were taught that healthy families are designed to support each other, protect each other, love each other, and encourage each other. Being a part of a family is critical. It means facing the world with the strength that the family bond brings. Families help shoulder the burdens and celebrate the successes. However, all that love and support can be twisted when one of the family members has an addiction. What once was just a very natural part of family members helping each other can morph into an enabling dysfunction where family members take over activities that their loved one should be able to handle on their own.

Looking back on our experience with Danielle, I felt the scales fall off my eyes. When Danielle had trouble in her relationships, I would step in to fix it. When Danielle made bad financial decisions, we would talk about the wise use of our resources, but I would often give her a little bit more money. She would rarely feel the pain. How many times had I come up with an action plan instead of letting my daughter develop her own problem-solving skills? And how many times had I rescued her to shield her from the true consequences of her actions? School, car, money, job, life—I never hesitated to swoop in and help. I thought I was doing a great job of loving her. The hard truth was that I was doing a great job of enabling her.

I thought I was doing a great job of loving my daughter. The hard truth was that I was doing a great job of enabling her.

One of the most life-changing sessions of the week was the discussion on whether alcoholism was a choice or a disease. There's still a raging debate on that issue. Is it a choice? Is it a disease? It gets complicated. Is it a choice that leads to a disease? Is it a disease that leads to a choice? What comes first, the chicken or the egg?

The argument that alcoholism is a choice goes something like this: It's a choice, and you need to learn to make better choices. Discover the triggers. Evaluate the outcomes. Develop self-control. Make better decisions. The concern is that if you think it's a disease, it absolves you from personal responsibility.

You will never get better because you will use your illness as an excuse. "I can't help myself. It's not my fault. I'm just sick."

There is an overwhelming amount of scientific and clinical evidence, however, that alcoholism is a disease. As I sat in the session, I remembered an experience I had just a few days prior.

I was getting a haircut when I overheard a conversation taking place in the chair next to mine. The hairstylist was talking openly with a client who was a recovering alcoholic. In her conversation, the client used the word *disease* to describe her condition. She then went on to say how understanding that she had a predisposition to alcoholism really empowered her to stay sober. She understood that just like people born with a heart condition may need to learn how to navigate life with that disability, she was born with an alcoholic disability, and she needed to learn how to navigate life without alcohol. It was her understanding that alcoholism is a disease that gave her the strength to choose a different life.

That's exactly the point the teacher was making in this session. Helping addicts see alcoholism as a disease does not absolve them from personal responsibility. It's simply the recognition that alcohol is poison to their body. The way their bodies respond to alcohol is not the same way other people's bodies respond. The way they're wired causes them to lose complete control, and because of that, they should never drink.

After Danielle had her alcohol-induced accident, I sat her down, and with all of the sincerity in my heart, I told her she could call me anytime, anywhere, and that I'd pick her up, no questions asked. I was emotional. I said it with tears. I wanted to remove all the barriers. Her life was more important to me than making her feel bad for a foolish choice.

She looked back up at me, and I'll never forget her words. "I would never call you," she said. "Don't get me wrong, I would *love* to call you. It's just that when alcohol hits my body, I go from zero to a hundred. When I drink, I always drink past my ability to reason. I have a disease. I can't drink like other people. I lose all control. I wish I could call you. I would love to be able to call you. I just wouldn't. When I drink, I get drunk."

Her response was the final nail in the coffin. I knew now that we were dealing with a killer, a disease intent on destroying my daughter. For Danielle, drinking was not just a choice. It was much deeper than that.

A few weeks later, I overheard Danielle's uncle asking her if she could ever see herself becoming a casual drinker. She replied, "For me, to drink is to die." I'm not sure when Danielle came to this realization, but I can't tell you how grateful I was to hear it. Drinking for Danielle was a matter of life and death, a fight to the finish with a relentless disease.

Is drinking a choice? Or is drinking a disease? Well, it's sort of both. It's a disease of choice. What starts as a choice becomes a disease, and every day Danielle would have to make the choice to live in a way that managed the disease and kept her healthy.

The last session of Family Week was all about giving family members the opportunity to express love, forgiveness, and encouragement to each other. It was very moving, with lots of raw emotions. Addicts asking for forgiveness and committing to a life of sobriety. Family members forgiving and pledging support. There was also a time when those in rehab could make requests of their family members as to how they could best support them post-rehab on their journey to recovery.

When Danielle's turn came to share, she asked us to pray for her and to celebrate her progress with joy. That was something we could do wholeheartedly. She then asked us to bury forever the thought that we did something wrong or that we weren't good enough parents. That touched on a pretty sensitive emotional nerve. I wish it were that easy. I knew that God was a perfect parent, and Adam and Eve still made bad choices. But often we observe respectful, overachieving kids and say, "They were raised right" or "Their parents did a great job with them." I felt such a strong sense of responsibility over Danielle and her struggles. *Surely if I had done a better job at parenting, we wouldn't be here, right?*

Truthfully, parents do play a role in how their children turn out. Love, support, encouragement, and wisdom play a huge role in a child's development. Still, life is complicated, and each of us is both a product of our environments and someone with the power to choose our own paths. Danielle's words forced me to see that, and I deeply appreciated her insight.

— *Danielle* —

When I first laid eyes on my family, I felt like I was in the twilight zone. It is easy to get familiar with rehab, but when you see people who are living in the real world—the world you came from and are eventually going back to—you become painfully aware that your rehab life is atypical.

My sweet, incredible, and unashamed family showed up to Family Week with the hats I had made them for Christmas. Seeing them in those terribly ugly hats warmed my heart, especially seeing one on my fashion-loving mom. It was definitely an unabashed expression of true love on their part. I hugged them tight.

I was nervous about the week ahead, but I was ready. *Here we go . . .*

Day one was eye-opening. We sat in a room full of strangers who felt like family. There was something about our common denominator that connected us. Everyone in the room was directly or indirectly affected by addiction. We heard countless versions of the same story. The bottom line was . . .

Nobody expected to end up there.
Everybody had open wounds.
Everybody had a part to play.

One of the biggest lessons we learned during Family Week was that addiction is a family disease. Everyone plays a role in it. Understanding your role is pivotal to long-term recovery, and I'm not just talking about the addict's long-term recovery. The codependent's or enabling parent's recovery is just as important. Understanding your role in the disease does not shift the blame to you, nor does it absolve the addict from their responsibilities.

It is simply equipping the family with the tools they need to heal and support the addict in their recovery.

On the last day of Family Week, we had to create a list of hurts. We had to look our loved ones in the eye and tell them exactly what they had done to hurt us. This felt so unnatural to me. I felt like I should be the only one to blame here. Remember, our family isn't very good at digging deep. We like to stay on Optimism Avenue.

For hours, I racked my brain, trying to come up with this list. I didn't really know what to say, but I knew this was a time that was very important. You can't get healing if you ignore your wounds.

I can honestly say I didn't have the more common wounds of feeling unloved or unwanted, or even any memories of times when my family said something mean. My wounds were a little bit different—more indirect. After spending hours searching my heart, I realized a few things—things that couldn't necessarily be changed. To be honest, I wasn't really sure if sharing them would do any good.

As a PK (pastor's kid), you live your life in a spotlight. It doesn't matter if your church is big or small—an entire body of people feels connected to you. They watch you, and they judge you. No matter what happens in your life, bad or good, people see it happen and they all have opinions about it. From a very young age, I learned to put out there the image I wanted people to see, the image of a normal life. A secret life became my best friend. I had very few people I could trust with my real self. Only a handful of people actually knew me, despite the large number of people who assumed they did. This reality hit the hardest when we lost Caleb. Grieving publicly is not an easy thing to do.

I realized I had some resentment about growing up as a preacher's kid. It felt stupid to even say out loud, but it was real for me. I thought maybe my parents did not consider how choosing that profession would affect their kids. Even if they never said it out loud, we were supposed to act a certain way. It was hard to share with them that their sacrifice and willingness to do God's will caused hurt in my life. It wasn't all bad, but that didn't change the truth of the wound.

I shared this with them, and they completely understood. They apologized from the deepest parts of their soul, not because they had done anything wrong, but for the very real pain they had caused me. It was such a beautiful moment to be heard and validated.

The honesty overflowed. It became apparent that many unexposed wounds had piled up over the years and that dealing with them all at once was overwhelming. I had to hear my parents tell me that even though they really wanted to trust me again, they knew it would be hard. What killed me even more was learning that as a result of my manipulation, they found it hard to even trust themselves.

I expressed to them how much pressure I felt to keep a "perfect" image alive after losing Caleb. I never wanted them to feel pain from their children again. Plus, I felt like I reminded them so much of him that I was responsible to keep his spirit alive. It was intense. All of these honest feelings hit us like an avalanche.

Family Week was tough, but it brought so much healing. It showed me how powerful it is to be gut-wrenchingly honest. I walked away feeling closer to my family and hopeful that we would have what it took to move toward long-term healing and recovery.

chapter seven

Sober Living

— *Danielle* —

After Family Week was over, the countdown began. I had only two weeks left before I would reenter the world. At first it didn't seem real to me. I had been in rehab for so long that the reality of an actual existence outside it seemed like a distant dream— and I constantly found myself dreaming of that day. I was so eager to begin my life and watch my dreams turn to reality.

I had been waiting a long time for this. We all had. Many of my cohorts had their own dreams and excitement. One of my friends couldn't wait to get out, determined to repair the trust she broke with her fiancé. One woman felt confident that she now had what it took to be the mother her children deserved. Another friend was in the middle of getting her degree and couldn't wait to apply her newfound motivation to her education. Our dreams were very real to us because for the last three months, they were all we had to get us through. We were bursting with the desire to make our dreams reality!

But as the day grew closer, the truth set in that we no longer had to dream. We were forced to consider our lives outside of these very familiar walls.

In my last week, my counselor asked me to make an agenda of what a typical week would look like on the outside, and this task brought me back to the real world. I had dreamed since day one of what it would be like to get out, but those dreams were so big that they didn't really cover the mundane realities of the first week out of rehab. I dreamed of changing the world and being an inspiration to others. But I couldn't get there without hard work and a day-to-day commitment to make my sobriety and recovery a priority. Again, I had to focus on the day in front of me, taking my sobriety one day at a time.

My first step to planning life after rehab was deciding where I was going to live. They suggested that for a higher chance of success in sobriety, I needed to transition to a sober living home. A sober living home is a place where you have a real job, real friends, a real car, and a real life within an environment of accountability and other women who are walking the journey toward recovery with you. It was a safe next step.

I picked a sober living home that I thought was the best fit, and having this decision secured gave me a lot of peace. Honestly, up to that point, though excited, I was really nervous about the real world, because the last time I was in the real world, my life was a mess. I felt like I had been given a second chance, and I didn't want anything to ruin this new beginning.

The next step was finding Twelve-Step meetings near me. At that point in my recovery, I was very familiar with AA and *The Big Book* of Alcoholics Anonymous. If you ever wonder if you have a drinking problem, read the first few chapters of *The BB* and you'll find your answer. The whole AA movement essentially outlines a twelve-step program to freedom.

AA meetings used to make me uncomfortable, but as I went through rehab and truly accepted my condition, I started to love them. There is something about sitting in a room of people who have screwed up the same way you have that makes you feel a sense of unity and togetherness. With AA, I felt like no matter where I was in the world, I could find a group of people just like me. So I researched groups near my sober living site and planned to attend every day.

The morning of my last day in rehab, I popped up, wide-eyed, absolutely beyond myself with excitement. The women I was closest with had already left, so I was genuinely ready to leave. There was not an ounce of sadness in my being.

I stood anxiously by the window waiting for my family to arrive. Every car that wasn't theirs felt like the universe playing a cruel trick on me. Finally, my anxiety calmed as I saw that oh-so-familiar, beautiful, white SUV roll around the corner. I am not a jumper, but I think I got a good two feet off the ground when I saw them.

I said my good-byes to the rehab team with a grin I couldn't even pretend to hide. My ride was here, ready to take me to my brand-new life!

—— *Rob* ——

Laura and I could feel Danielle's excitement. She was ready to get out. The counselors were sure that Danielle had taken full advantage of what the program had to offer. I was grateful, and we were cautiously optimistic. We could see some of the changes in Danielle that we had been praying for. In the last few weeks, she had taken some leadership responsibilities with the incoming program participants by showing them the ropes and making them feel at home. Now she seemed confident, more sure of herself, and ready to tackle the next step. It was hard to believe that this was the same girl who nervously walked onto the campus three months earlier.

The last few conversations with her counselors were filled with information about the next steps after rehab. We were told over and over about how critical this transition was. We were warned not to be deceived into thinking that Danielle was now cured of her addictions. They told us to remain vigilant, to keep our guard up. Danielle would have to fight every day for her sobriety.

Laura and I were thankful that Danielle was progressing, but it's not easy living with the thought that at any moment this whole journey could unravel. Words and phrases like *fight, keep your guard up*, and *stay vigilant* sound good in a conversation, but they're hard to live out. I hated the thought that a person never really gets over addiction. I'm still not sure how I feel about that. Sometimes I wished I could just snap my fingers and never have to be concerned about her again, but life doesn't work that way. Most of the time, we were up for the challenge, but sometimes we felt tired and emotionally spent.

Transitioning out of rehab is not easy, and in some ways this was the most difficult step in the recovery process. When addicts are released from rehab, there is a real danger of relapse. Going from a highly structured environment where no alcohol and drugs are permitted on the property to a new living arrangement where you can participate in your addiction of choice is a very vulnerable time. I pictured Olympic athletes in a relay race. Passing the baton safely is the most important and challenging part of the race. And passing the baton from rehab to normal life is infinitely more important and challenging.

Everyone we talked to was adamant about Danielle not returning to our home. Instead, they strongly encouraged us to consider a supervised sober living home. Their reasoning was based on their experience that home, no matter how supportive and loving, was filled with triggers that could be problematic. The best course of action was to start her post-rehab journey in a new environment with a trained supervisor who would know what to look for and could provide the support she would need.

I had no idea what a sober living home was, so I had to do some research. Typically, they are homes ranging from three to five bedrooms, with one room reserved for the supervisor and the others dedicated to recovering addicts. Depending on the size of the home, each room has three to five beds. The refrigerator is divided into sections, with each person responsible for their own meals and cleanup. The houses are gender specific. There are a few rules, which apply to everyone. There's a zero-tolerance policy concerning drugs and alcohol. One violation and you're out. No exceptions! No excuses! You also have to keep your room clean. Find a job. Find a sponsor. Be home by curfew. And participate in nightly recovery meetings. The structure of the sober living home felt right to Laura and me, and it seemed like the next right step.

We were encouraged to finalize her arrangements before her last day at rehab so she could move right in. After extensive investigation, phone interviews, and talking with Danielle, we settled on what we all thought was the best option. Just for a final confirmation, Laura and I scheduled an appointment to meet with the sober living supervisor and to check out the neighborhood and living arrangements.

That day turned out to be one of the most emotional days of the entire recovery journey.

I put the address into the phone app and started the forty-five-minute journey across town. The GPS led us to what looked like the most dangerous and drug-infested part of town. I pulled the car over, and we just stared at the place where our daughter was going to live for the next year of her life. I started to imagine Danielle walking past drug dealers, being a potential target for violent thieves, and having to defend herself from unwanted advances. I pictured Laura and me tossing and turning every night, wondering if our daughter would be safe.

One look at Laura, and I could tell she was madder than I'd ever seen her. Pastors or not, we're still human, and the conversation that flowed was filled with a few four-letter expletives that never in a million years I would've thought could come from my wife's mouth. "If you think I'm going to allow my daughter to live here, you're absolutely crazy," she said in a very sanitized version of the story. Something about the rawness in her words gave me the freedom to express my own, and in a conversation where we sounded more like sailors than pastors, we had a complete emotional breakdown.

In a span of fifteen minutes we voiced our anger at everything and everyone. We threw a pity party. We were upset with our counselors, who recommended such an obviously inappropriate place. We were frustrated with Danielle, who put us where we were in the first place. We were disappointed with God, who didn't step in earlier and protect her. How were we supposed to trust God with her sobriety if she was going to be living in a place like this? We even turned on each other with some version of the "if we had been better parents, this wouldn't have happened" story. It was brutal, and we felt at a total loss. This neighborhood and this house were almost physical embodiments of the pain, disappointment, and fear that hid in the darkest corners of our hearts.

After our meltdown, I happened to glance at the GPS and realized I had entered the wrong address.

We laugh about it now, but it wasn't funny back then. Thankfully, when I entered the correct address, we found ourselves in a really nice neighborhood. We both breathed a huge sigh of relief. Not only that, but at the house we had an absolutely delightful conversation with the supervisor, who gained our trust immediately. At the end of the day, we drove home embarrassed and emotionally drained, but grateful.

When we picked up Danielle from rehab on her final day, we stopped off at our house to collect a few more things for her twelve months in the sober living home. Once Danielle had what she needed, we put the correct address in the GPS, drove there, and got her settled into her new home.

— *Danielle* —

My mind was racing a million miles an hour on the drive from rehab to the sober living home. I was excited to meet my new roommates, as well as see my closest friend from rehab, who had moved in the week before. I knew that what was ahead wasn't going to be easy, but in that moment, I was optimistic.

We pulled up to a nice house with a million cars in front of it. It was a decent-sized house, but it definitely didn't seem big enough to handle as many people as there were cars represented. I walked in and was greeted by nine lovely girls. I was happy to see so many smiling faces, but I also began to wonder where we were all going to sleep. You have no idea the level of Tetris that went into fitting that many beds into one room! I was impressed and a tad claustrophobic. Nonetheless, I was excited to start my new life.

Just like rehab, there were rules. Though I was happy to have the accountability, I was even happier that these rules seemed a bit more reasonable. The wake-up call was 7:30 a.m. during the week for morning meditation, and we had to attend five AA meetings a week. We each would be responsible for a daily chore. And every Sunday, we'd be drug-tested in order to maintain accountability.

During rehab, I had missed going to my home church. Now I would finally have the opportunity to go back, and I eagerly counted down the days.

When I walked into church that first Sunday, I felt immediately at home. Everything looked and smelled the same, and I was comforted by its familiarity. While being a PK had its downsides, I also felt like this place was family—my church had helped raise me, and I felt safe here.

As happy as I was to return to such a familiar, grace-filled space, I still had responsibilities. My sober living house required that I get a job within two weeks. This made me nervous. Up to that point, life had been handed to me on a platter. For the first time, I had to find a job all on my own. *You mean I can't call my dad?* I felt lost. I didn't know if I had anything to contribute to a company. Insecurity gripped me.

With God's grace and a lot of uncomfortable interviews and conversations, I got a job at a local accounting firm as a receptionist. It wasn't what I wanted to do with the rest of my life, but I can't even put into words how fulfilling it was to make my own way. I'll admit, I was learning this adult thing a little late in life, but hey, better late than never.

—— *Rob* ——

While Laura and I rejoiced at the progress that Danielle was making in her recovery, this next step to a sober living home brought back a flood of concerns. It didn't take long for me to realize that rehab, with its "lockdown" security, had afforded me three months of real peace. I was absolutely confident that as long as Danielle was in rehab, she was not doing drugs or drinking. Now that she was out, I didn't have the same level of confidence, and I found it hard to trust. Just prior to rehab, my confidence in Danielle's truthfulness was at an all-time low. To be completely blunt, Danielle, as an addict, was a phenomenal liar. With her facial expressions and tone of voice, she was able to paint the picture she wanted me to see, even if it had no basis in reality. She was a skilled manipulator too, taking full advantage of the father-daughter bond to get what she wanted. After so many lies and deceptions, how could I believe her now?

For whatever reason, Laura has always had a better read on our kids than I ever did. Most of the time, I wanted to believe the best, while Laura often argued that more investigation and discernment were needed. In retrospect, she was clearly right. But now I found myself wondering if I would believe the truth even if it was staring me in the face. I decided that maybe the best thing to do was to have a truly frank conversation with Danielle about my lack of ability to trust.

I asked Danielle about the times she said that everything was great when they weren't. We talked about the times she flat-out lied about her drinking. We discussed the made-up stories and her ability to manipulate our perception of her. I shared with her that because of our past, I was having trouble with my confidence to discern when she was telling the truth.

Danielle heard me out, and she didn't blame me one bit.

She completely understood and gave me the freedom to ask any question at any time until the trust in our relationship was restored. Not only that, but she gave us the freedom to talk to her friends, counselors, and anyone who would be in the know. She wanted us to be assured that the changes we were seeing and hoping for were real. She wanted truth with us as much as we wanted it with her.

As we journeyed together with Danielle in this new phase of her recovery, we wanted to build our relationship on truth, because that was the only way trust could be restored. But I also had to face my own issues with truth. Maybe I was so easily deceived because I *wanted* to be. Part of me didn't want to face the reality that I had a daughter who was addicted to drugs and alcohol, so I had lied to myself and lived in denial, justifying her behavior with lies and excuses very similar to the ones that addicts tell themselves. I needed to change, to face my own tendency to create a false reality. In order to change, I had to live in the truth too. As Jesus himself said, "You will know the truth, and the truth will set you free" (John 8:32).

— *Danielle* —

If there's one thing that exists 100 percent of the time in the life of an addict, it is *lying.* You can be a liar without being an addict, but you can't be an addict without being a liar. Lying is an inevitable part of the equation.

There's a false perception that people become more honest

when they're drunk, that their true colors show. That is not actually true. In reality, when your body is taken over by another substance, you are no longer yourself. You no longer have judgment. You no longer have the ability to discern the truth, nor the ability to make decisions based on truth. While this most certainly does not absolve a person from any behavior committed while intoxicated, I can see why a life of lies is necessary for an addict. I have woken up so many mornings entirely embarrassed about my actions from the night before. As a result of that embarrassment, I felt the need to lie to protect any piece of my true self I had left.

Addicts lie to others and to themselves so often that they forget the difference between lies and reality.

Addicts lie for many reasons. When addiction is in full effect, we see red. Alcohol is something we crave, something we need in order to function. We're desperate for it and will do anything to get it. Truth is no longer a priority, and honestly, it is not even a thought at that point. Lying becomes an art, essential to maintaining our lifestyle.

We lie by hiding alcohol all over our house. We lie and say, "Work kept me late" when we are really at the bar. We lie to ourselves, saying, "This is just a phase" or "I deserve it." We lie. Lying to maintain our addiction leads to an addiction to lying itself. We start to forget the difference between our lies and reality. We have lied to others and even ourselves for so long that it all kind of blends together. We start to lie for no reason. If I ate a hotdog for lunch, I might lie and say I ate a hamburger. Why? I have no earthly idea. Maybe I think you're a person who prefers hamburgers to hotdogs and I don't want you to dislike me. It is plain and simple—addicts are liars.

Another piece of truth that you have to embrace is all the pain you have caused and all the trust you have broken. It is much easier for you to forget the mistakes you made than it is for those you hurt. So even when your life is starting to get better, there is still some relational wreckage left behind.

Usually a simple apology won't work. Most of the time, you have to repair relational damage by living your amends, and that means it will take time. There is no shortcut to earning trust back; believe me, I have searched. Instead, I had to decide daily to put others before myself. I had to dedicate myself to hard work, to taking responsibility for my own life. And I had to be honest about where I had been.

Recovery demands honesty, because truth is the fabric that holds our integrity together. Coming to terms with the truth was brutal; honestly, it still is brutal. It takes constant awareness and inventory of my heart to stay honest. But the truth is, my sobriety depends on it. Sober living is a process of gradual change, not a place of finished perfection. Who knew that living authentically, soberly, would take so much work?

chapter eight

Who Am I?

—— *Rob* ——

Now that Danielle was out of rehab, I found myself stumbling over the same temptations. I wanted to step in and keep her close. If it hadn't been for the strong advice of her counselors, I would have brought her home after rehab. I was also fighting the urge to help her get a job. We had thousands of contacts in Austin. Should we make a few phone calls? Should we make it easy? But remembering I have a tendency to enable Danielle, and remembering her request during Family Week, I stepped aside and let her make her own way. We would provide all the love, encouragement, and prayers, but she would have to walk this one out herself.

Given Danielle's carefree approach to life, I was surprised at the job she landed. I would have never pictured her in an accounting office, but she found that job all on her own. It was a small victory for both of us.

Our schedule found a new rhythm. Laura and I continued to work hard at church, and Danielle's life was also super busy. She had to wake up at 7:00 a.m. to get ready and make the drive across town in heavy traffic. Between her get-togethers with the girls in her sober living home and support groups in the community, she had meetings every night. The only thing that seemed different from rehab was that we saw her at church on the weekends and we got to communicate by phone anytime we wanted. We asked lots of questions every day. And she patiently answered each and every one as we slowly and carefully rebuilt trust.

With some type of recovery meeting required nightly, Danielle had to research to find meetings that matched her schedule. There were two major organizations to choose from: church-based groups most often affiliated with Celebrate Recovery and community-based groups most often affiliated with AA. There were tons of similarities. They both followed a twelve-step program. They both used chips to mark and celebrate sobriety milestones. They both used small groups to share their stories and encourage each other. But there were also some differences. And one small difference provided Danielle and me with some talking points for a huge issue. An issue so big that it's at the core of every decision we make. How is that for *big*?

The issue? *Identity*. The topic came up when Danielle noticed the difference in how people introduced themselves in the two settings. In AA, Danielle would hear people say, "Hello, my name is John, and I am an alcoholic." Meanwhile, in Celebrate Recovery, she would hear people say, "Hello, my name is John, and I am struggling with alcohol."

At first glance, it may be easy to blow off the difference as semantics. No big deal, right? They basically mean the same thing. They're both trying to communicate that alcohol is a huge issue in their lives and they're learning to manage the challenges and live with victory over it. But there really were significant implications in the difference. As Danielle and I talked about it, we found some things we liked about both approaches. In the AA tradition, by confessing, "I am an alcoholic," the person is recognizing that addiction is a huge challenge, and they will never be able to let their guard down. It will be a battle they'll face for the rest of their lives.

In the Celebrate Recovery tradition, group members embraced the lifelong challenge of addiction, but they also embraced the supernatural work done on the cross by Jesus, the Son of God, that changed forever the issue of their identity. When someone puts their faith in Jesus, they are never again identified by their behavior. Instead, their identity is found *in Christ.* Second Corinthians 5:17 reads, "Therefore, if anyone is in Christ, the new creation has come: The old has gone, the new is here!"

Those who put their faith in Christ are not drug addicts or alcoholics. They may be struggling with those issues, but that is not who they are. So people in the recovery group that meets at our church say something like this: "Hello, my name is Danielle. I am a grateful believer in the Lord Jesus Christ, and I am struggling with alcohol."

As Danielle and I dialogued about this issue of identity, we tapped into some of the real reasons her life got off track.

Fundamentally, she didn't see herself the way God did. She saw herself as "less than," as not good enough. Because of that, she did what all of us do—she *behaved* out of what she *believed*. She believed she was less than those around her and needed alcohol to become a better version of herself, so that's how she lived. Bad beliefs about identity lead to bad behavior, and bad behavior exacerbates bad beliefs, creating a vicious downward spiral.

Identity is everything.

We behave out of what we believe about ourselves.

In Numbers 13, the story is told about the Israelites' struggle to enter Canaan, the land God had promised them. After Moses sent out twelve spies to get the lay of the land, they came back with their report: "We went into the land to which you sent us, and it does flow with milk and honey! Here is its fruit. But the people who live there are powerful, and the cities are fortified and very large" (Numbers 13:27–28). All of the spies, except Joshua and Caleb, believed that the land—though fertile and desirable—could not be conquered.

The most poignant point of the story, however, was not how powerful the opposition was; it was how the ten spies saw themselves. They reported, "We can't attack those people; they are stronger than we are . . . We seemed like grasshoppers in our own eyes, and we looked the same to them" (Numbers 13:31–33). They refused to enter the Promised Land because they saw themselves as insignificant little bugs—grasshoppers. Because they saw themselves in the worst light possible, they gave up and turned their backs on God and his plan for their lives.

The Israelites are not the only ones who think of themselves as grasshoppers. All of us do at one time or another. I know I did. On and off during this entire process, I felt like a "grass-hopper" parent. I have always been a pretty confident, "can do" kind of guy, but this experience crushed me. What did I do wrong? Or more to the point, *what was wrong with me?* I felt defeated more times than I cared to admit, and my bad beliefs produced some bad behaviors.

I lost confidence not just in my parenting but in other areas of life, like leadership and vision casting. I found myself talking negative and expecting the worst. I had to come to grips with the truth that I am not my roles. My identity is not pastor, husband, or father. My identity is in Christ. Before anything else, I am a beloved son of Almighty God. Nothing else about me even comes close in terms of significance. And nothing can take that away.

—— *Danielle* ——

Picture this for a minute . . .

Imagine me as a little girl with innocent, wide, brown eyes and a smile that can brighten up any room. I walked confidently wherever I went, talking to every person who walked by. To me, there was no such thing as a stranger. I trusted the world I lived in; it had been kind to me.

I lived with this unbroken confidence for years. Until one day, when I was ten years old, a typical coming-of-age thing happened to me: I started to notice the boys in my class.

This was normal. Except that I was just a little bit heavier than the other girls; the other girls seemed to get noticed back, and I didn't. I wondered why this was. It didn't make sense to me. Up until that very moment, I had never questioned my worth. That day my identity changed.

Even though I didn't quite understand why, I believed the lie that something about me wasn't enough. That marked the beginning of my endless pursuit to obtain the thing I believed I lacked.

I snuck out and went to a house party for the first time when I was sixteen. At that party I drank and danced, hoping to claim the attention of any young man. Still searching for that thing I lacked. This led to one guy pressing boundaries I never wanted to cross.

I was violated and ashamed, believing more than ever that who I was did not match society's standards. On the outside it looked like I was fine. I had friends; I wasn't alone. It appeared that I belonged, but that couldn't be further from the truth of how I felt on the inside.

I soon discovered that something could quickly activate in me the things I believed I lacked. I drank to become exciting, witty, and vivacious. I took Adderall to make me focused and determined. I smoked weed to relax. I threw up most of my meals to get skinny. I had figured out the perfect system, each part working in what I thought was perfect harmony.

I had found a shortcut to my dreams. All I ever wanted was to be accepted for who I was, but there was no longer an ounce of my real self in sight.

By the end of my addiction days, my sense of identity was very poor.

I believed I was unworthy.

I believed I wasn't enough.

I believed I was getting what I deserved.

I believed I was unlovable.

I believed I was a failure.

I believed other people were better than me.

I was physically, emotionally, and spiritually defeated. Believing those things about myself made it very difficult to get out of the cycle I was in. That is how I knew it was completely God's grace that pulled me out. Sin and shame consumed me. I no longer believed I was an imperfect human who messed up; I believed I was an imperfect human who *was* my mistakes.

At that point, my identity was broken, but it wasn't until sobriety that I actually had to face what I believed about myself. In the past when negative emotions and thoughts crept up, I would self-medicate them away. I didn't have that option in sobriety. We dealt with some major issues in rehab, but only when I got back into the real world did it become abundantly clear that I had no idea who I was. That was a terrifying realization. How does one discover who they are, especially this late in the game?

Rehab was a safe, highly structured place, so being faced with the responsibility of making my own decisions again was unsettling. I had no guarantee of long-term sobriety. For the last five years, my identity had been drugs and alcohol.

In rehab, I was the rehab girl. Now all of a sudden, I had the rest of my life ahead of me, and I had no idea what I wanted or even who I was.

I didn't know what my hobbies were. I didn't have the friends I once had. I didn't know the direction I wanted my life to go. It was a very confusing time for me, and it felt like my self-discovery years were behind me. But that wasn't true. I may have been getting a later start, but I still had so much to discover about myself, with the rest of my life to do it.

One morning, it dawned on me that I didn't need to start from scratch. God whispered to my heart to embrace life like I did when I was a child, reminding me that the confidence and innocence of a child is always how he intends for us to live. Memories flooded my heart of the young, tenacious adventurer I once was. I realized that deep down, that is who I am— confident, adventurous, determined, motivated, comforting, kind, and, most important, unconditionally loved.

I knew it would take a lifetime to learn all of who I am, so I removed that pressure. But what I could do was discern what *isn't* true about me. I had accepted so many things as a part of my identity that *weren't* true. So I needed to take the things I believed about myself and line them up with the truth of God's Word.

This search for my true identity helped me find a recovery program that worked for me. Both AA and Celebrate Recovery focus on community and healing, but the idea of one's identity is very different in the two groups. While AA has participants identify themselves by their name and the admission that they are an alcoholic, Celebrate Recovery's preferred introduction style doesn't allow you to define yourself by your issues. Rather, it puts a person's identity and worth in Christ while they struggle with their issues.

I think understanding the seriousness of addiction is invaluable, and for some people, admitting they are indeed an alcoholic reminds them that to drink is to die. I have to believe alcoholism is an incurable disease that I can treat daily, but at the same time I know I am not my mistakes. By God's grace I am free, and I feel uncomfortable professing anything over my life other than the fact that I am a child of God.

Coming to terms with my identity as a child of God would, and still does, combat a lifetime of negative thinking. It also unlocked the realization that nothing I have ever done or ever will do can separate me from who I really am—a child of God.

——— *Rob* ———

Danielle had heard me preach her entire life. She knew the message that defined the heartbeat of the Bible—the beauty of God's amazing grace. I wanted Danielle to really believe in her heart of hearts what Christianity was all about. I wanted her to know that God loved her no matter what, that he would always forgive her, and that he would never leave her or forsake her, no matter how many promises and pledges she had broken. And I wanted her to be forever convinced that, as a gift of his amazing grace and love, God gave her a new identity. She was not a grasshopper. She was not less than. She was a beloved, brand-spanking-new child of God.

It would take courage to believe that.

When Danielle was much younger, I would grab her face with my hands, gently put my nose on her nose, and tell her how much I loved her and what an incredible treasure she was to me. Now that Danielle was twenty, she was not quite as comfortable with my face being that close to hers. But for old time's sake, I grabbed her face with my hands, put my nose on her nose, and said, "Danielle, never forget that you are the beloved daughter of Almighty God. That is who you really are!"

It takes courage to believe that.

chapter nine

The Danger Zone

— *Danielle* —

Recovery, if you choose it, can be the most life-giving process you will ever walk through. It can and does work, if you let it.

However, as addicts we have this one daunting, lingering thing that is waiting to pounce on us at any given moment. It seeks out our most vulnerable moments, constantly searching for any opportunity to sink its claws in deep. What is that danger? *Relapse.*

Relapse, unfortunately, is a very real threat for addicts. When you're at the beginning of your recovery journey, the future seems bright. Relapse is the farthest thing from your mind, but it can sneak up on anyone. Every single one of my group of women in rehab had dreams we wanted to achieve, and we all had hope that this thing was going to work. We didn't dismiss the hard work it would take, but I promise you that none of us considered ourselves weak enough to relapse. We internalized what we learned and thought, *How could it not work?* Even looking back now, I truly remember believing that every girl in that room was going to make it. What I don't think everyone realized is that recovery is a *lifelong*, day-to-day process.

The truth is that *no one* is immune from relapse. Just because you make the choice at one point in time to choose sobriety doesn't indefinitely secure your spot in long-term recovery. I wish it did. But it doesn't.

I vividly recall the moment I first heard of a friend's relapsing. This friend—we'll call him Jon—was active in AA and seemed to be living his best life. He was doing well, and he had goals he was working to achieve. But as time went on, I saw less and less of him. Still, I always assumed the best. After all, if anyone could make it in recovery, it'd be Jon.

Jon relapsed.

That shook me to my core. I could hardly believe it until I heard the words straight from his mouth. Jon is a really good guy, one of the best I know, and he wasn't immune. What a stunningly painful reality check.

After Jon, it felt like they were dropping like flies. Brittany, my closest friend from rehab, and I kept hearing story after story of all our sisters caught in relapse after relapse. Around six months after we left rehab, only a few of us were left in the sober game. It seemed that the common story, as time went on, was that people started to believe they were cured. They started to believe they could handle life on their own. First this assumption seemed harmless; they simply stopped coming to AA meetings or stopped connecting with their community. Then their isolation grew stronger. They started believing that maybe one drink or one hit couldn't hurt. They believed that now they could handle it. They believed they could do meth like a lady or take shots like a gentleman. Oh, the lies we believe!

As time flew by, the already small circle grew smaller. By the time I hit my one year of sobriety, only Brittany and I hadn't relapsed.

I was forced to wonder what was different about Brittany and me. Why hadn't we relapsed? Then it dawned on me that we weren't running this race alone. I'm not talking about having each other, though that was certainly helpful. I'm talking about a relationship with Jesus.

The whole AA movement is extremely spiritual, and it in no way talks down on Christianity, but it also allows any type of spiritual connection. That can sound attractive to people who were burned by the church. It makes sense when life has been so cruel to you that having faith in a loving God seems impossible. I get it. But just like tofu is no substitute for a juicy, 100 percent beef steak, there is no substitute for God, and he certainly played a big part in our recovery. Like me, Brittany was a believer, but the history of her faith had been rocky. In sobriety was the first time in a long time that she had truly given God a shot. Her faith wasn't perfect, but no one's is. She and I went to church every Sunday, and she had an eagerness to learn—and that was beautiful to me.

But as the months went by, Brittany and I started to go our

separate ways. Our friendship was interesting, as she was quite a bit older than me. She was a mother, and her sole purpose in sobriety was to reunite with her children. Meanwhile, I was still trying to figure out what my next step was going to be. I knew it wouldn't be forever that we lived in the same house and had the same schedule. Her kids didn't even live in Austin. So eventually we had to go our separate ways. At first, we stayed in touch often. She came to church every weekend. Her life seemed to be put together, and her recovery was still a priority.

But as time went on, I got more involved in church, and she started working. Then her work schedule conflicted with church. She made it every now and then, but I saw her less and less. I cared about her deeply, but our lives went in different directions. We talked every once in a while, but never for long, and the content was always surface level. Eventually the communication stopped. We had new circles. I checked in when I could, but I never really heard back.

She relapsed.

Brittany deserved a good life. She had done the hard work. She knew Jesus. For a time, she was connected.

But just like anyone can connect, anyone can disconnect.

My heart broke for my friend, and selfishly it broke for me too. I felt alone.

Isolation is a sure path straight to the danger zone.

But in this season, I learned something that transformed my life. I learned that when my circle is small, I need to pick up my pen and draw a bigger circle.

I didn't need to draw a bigger circle to leave people behind, but I was alone—and alone is not good. Remember, alone for me equals binge drinking by myself in my room. Isolation is a sure path straight to the danger zone.

—— *Rob* ——

Relapse was a huge challenge and an ever-present fear for us. There were fifteen other women who went through rehab with Danielle. Every one of them relapsed. *Every one!* We knew the statistics. According to various studies, Danielle had an 80 percent chance of relapse in the first year. If she was able to stay sober for one year, her relapse probabilities went down to 50 percent. If she was able to stay sober for five years, her relapse probabilities would go all the way down to 15 percent. The longer she remained sober, the more likely she would stay that way. I didn't like the odds at all. *An 80 percent fail rate in the first year! Are you kidding me?* And our experience of seeing all the people Danielle was connected with faltering, one right after another, made those statistics seem optimistic.

The thought that all of our hard work, sacrifice, and progress could slip away with a few bad choices was unnerving. We didn't even want to think about the possibility, but the statistics were being confirmed right before our eyes. At times like these, we would ask our friends and family to add their prayers alongside ours. I was so grateful not to be in this battle alone.

We knew this first year was huge. We didn't take anything for granted, and we didn't assume she was going to make it.

We prayed every day. We asked lots of questions. We loved on her the best we knew how. We watched for any sign that things were going sideways. And on May 15, we celebrated with joy her six months of sobriety.

Danielle and I talked frankly about being in this danger zone. Technically, relapse is defined as the process where someone eventually continues their drinking habits as they did before recovery. A relapse is not necessarily a one-drink slipup or mistake. But Danielle didn't even want the one-drink experience. The sober living home, the meetings, the Twelve Steps, the sponsor, the accountability, and the rehab were all about avoiding relapse.

The truth was, Danielle experienced multiple relapses before rehab. We knew what that felt like, and we never wanted to go through that again. As I thought about it, I could make the case that nobody gets to sobriety without experiencing relapse. That's how people discover they have a problem. They drink or do drugs. They commit to never doing it again. They relapse. They realize they need help. Obviously, however, the more a person relapses, the greater the consequences.

Recognizing the triggers to relapse is imperative because relapse is so dangerous. When people relapse after a period of sobriety, they tend to go a little bit deeper and longer than they did before. They find themselves with an addiction misery index much higher than anything they ever experienced previously. The health issues and relational wreckage become even more devastating. Repeated relapses lower a person's belief that they can actually stay sober and drains them of their desire to try. Motivation to change gets harder to find after each failure. And some become so depressed that they just give up on life completely. Family and friends, who have already suffered immensely, try to find the emotional reserves to fight again, but with each relapse, they struggle too. It was unnerving to contemplate the consequences.

Danielle seemed to be managing the relapse epidemic unfolding all around her with maturity and resolve. I was grateful, but I was also really concerned. The stats were like a huge blinking billboard in my mind. Eighty percent fail! Eighty percent relapse! I wasn't sure if my tender heart could take it if Danielle turned her back on recovery. It was hard to know the best way to help keep Danielle on the path to recovery, so I tried to learn as much as I could about the triggers that caused a relapse and shared my knowledge with Danielle.

Right from the start there were some practical "no-brainers" to avoid. Don't hang out with active substance abusers, and don't go to places where alcohol is being served. Danielle was passionately committed to avoiding those situations, but sometimes it got a little bit more complicated than just not going to bars or not hanging out with people who drank. What about family and friends who drank responsibly? What about going to restaurants and movie theaters that just happened to serve alcohol? Some gray areas needed to be navigated. Fortunately, Danielle's good friends and family were absolutely supportive and removed alcohol from any environment that Danielle would be a part of. But Danielle knew she wouldn't be able to avoid seeing alcohol completely. It was on the shelves of every grocery store and available at every gas station. Just being aware helped her avoid those temptations.

We sidestepped other relapse pitfalls by having a well-thought-out transition plan from the protective bubble of rehab to the vulnerability of normal everyday living. Every Monday night, we would meet at our house for dinner, games, and a time to pray for each other. I always looked forward to these evenings together so I could assess for myself how she was really doing.

Studies have shown that more than 90 percent of our communication is nonverbal. Being able to look in Danielle's eyes and hear the tone of her voice and observe her overall demeanor was huge for me. If she was down, I would give her extra attention. But more often than not, her joy and positive outlook would provide a huge emotional lift and quell my doubts. Every week, the bond of our trust grew stronger.

The other days of the week, when we wouldn't see her, were more problematic for me. The relapse protocols were less clear, not as easy to discern or monitor, because they mostly had to be managed by Danielle herself. It was hard for me to take a back seat in those instances, but I had to let Danielle take control of her own sobriety. Her counselors made sure she managed things like having unrealistic expectations surrounding her sobriety. Graduating from rehab was a start, not an end, and they wanted her to embrace the reality that there would be future struggles.

Some of the other causes behind relapse made me genuinely terrified, like the possibility that Danielle hadn't addressed the root cause of her addiction. How could we know if she had uncovered that or not? Or what if Danielle became so overwhelmed by something in her life that she turned to alcohol for comfort? I couldn't control those triggers, and often I had to fight my urge to smother her in my fear for her continued sobriety. The hardest part was learning to trust God and Danielle when I couldn't be there to protect or help her navigate through the ups and downs of life.

With all that said, we weren't completely unarmed. Our counselors and research gave us some signs we could be watching out for. We paid close attention to her overall outlook on life. Was she reasonably happy and optimistic, or anxious and depressed? We monitored her schedule. Was she missing meetings? Was she behaving secretively? Was she living isolated? We were really interested in her relationships. Was she hanging out with the right kind of people?

It was also super helpful to know the anatomy of a relapse. Relapse is seldom a single event but is instead most often a gradual process. In fact, a relapse usually begins weeks before any alcohol or drugs are abused. The recovery community identifies three stages of relapse: emotional, mental, and physical.

Relapse is seldom a single event but is instead most often a gradual process.

Almost all relapses start *emotionally.* Danielle, like most addicts, dealt with her negative emotions and feelings by abusing drugs and alcohol. Now that she was sober, she would need to rely on the coping techniques she learned over the last few months, because if she didn't deal with her emotions in a healthy way, she would be super vulnerable to the next stage of relapse. So she needed to journal her thoughts and emotions. She needed to dispel negative feelings by listening to good music. And she needed to talk to trusted allies, reaching out to her sponsor or attending a support group meeting whenever she felt her emotions going sideways. She was going to feel negative emotions from time to time. That was a given. But it was critical for her to recognize them and process them wisely.

If Danielle's emotions went unchecked, she could conceivably enter into the second stage—*mental* relapse. This would be the stage where Danielle would start thinking about the possibility of drinking. I wanted her to know, however, that just because she thought about it didn't mean she would do it or had done it. The enemy uses a devious strategy, whispering, "Since you've already thought about it, you've already crossed the line; you may as well do it." I didn't want Danielle to fall for that lie. The truth is that everyone thinks about doing stupid things. Even Jesus was tempted. But any addict who stays in the mental relapse stage too long will start putting themselves in risky situations and actually start thinking through and planning out a real physical relapse.

Danielle and I talked about the coping skills needed in this stage. I told her she would need to break the cycle in her thinking. Take a walk. Get some air. Change her environment or scenery so she could recalibrate her thinking and get reconnected with the big picture. And most of all, I encouraged her to share her feelings. "That's why you have sponsors, support groups, and family," I told her. I expressed as sincerely as I could that there would never be any judgment from us. She could talk to us about anything at any time, and we would do everything we could to help her.

The third stage is a real *physical* relapse. If Danielle was to reach this place, I told her we would just begin again. I told her she might feel lots of shame, disappointment, and hopelessness, but giving up was not an option. We would all have a good cry, go back to step one, and then go to step two. We would go all in. We would learn from our mistakes, and eventually we would overcome. No matter what, we would win.

What was really interesting to me was my own journey through these three stages. I wasn't in danger of relapsing into drugs and alcohol, but I was definitely relapsing into worry and fear. I had to do for myself exactly what I was encouraging Danielle to do. I had to learn to manage my own emotions.

I remember one Saturday afternoon when I was sitting on the back porch, tears running down my cheeks. I didn't even know why. We were doing well. Danielle was in a good place. Maybe the whole journey was just taking its toll. Sometimes I didn't know why I was feeling what I was feeling. But in those low times, I had to do what I encouraged Danielle to do. I talked with friends. I journaled my thoughts. I prayed. I went out for a walk and got some fresh air. I looked for ways to change my environment and reconnect with the big picture.

Of course I realize I had an advantage in that Danielle herself was fighting hard for her recovery. So many families didn't have that hope, that consolation . . . and my heart broke for them. Still, even when Danielle was doing well, I remembered the enormity of her fight—how it would be lifelong—and some-times I felt like giving up. I could live in the fog of discourage-ment for days, so I would have to go back to the beginning and realize I was powerless on my own to control my life. I would commit to going all in again, and I would reach for my Higher Power, Jesus.

— *Danielle* —

Even though I've been consecutively sober for four years, the truth is the only sobriety I really have is today. I only ever have the day I am currently in.

I am not immune.

Going to rehab doesn't make me immune.

Having great parents doesn't make me immune.

Not even writing this book makes me immune.

I would love to be able to press a button that will guarantee immunity for the rest of my life—that would be awesome.

But in reality, my only chance of staying sober each day is to stay continually aware of my condition. When I forget my condition, I can be sure that relapse is right around the corner, waiting for me.

I know I have said this before, but my story is not only for alcoholics or drug addicts. We all have weaknesses. We all have bad habits. We all have things that God has been continually asking us to lay down before him, but our pride won't let us. So please insert your own issues.

There are three things I need in my life not just to stay sober but to live in freedom:

- God
- community
- service

For the most part, in sobriety, I wasn't around alcohol. My family were never big drinkers, so it wasn't a huge stretch for them to not have it around. But as my circle grew bigger, the exposure grew. I had a ton of church friends who would have a beer occasionally.

I need three things in my life not just to stay sober but to live in freedom: God, community, and service.

While I know it's totally possible for someone to love the Lord and have a drink, at the same time, to this day it's still hard for me to understand how someone can have one glass and not have twenty more after that. Apparently casual drinking exists . . . still, it's so weird.

Being around the occasional beer after rehab didn't tempt me as much as it made me uncomfortable. I didn't crave it when I saw it, but it felt like seeing an old friend who stabbed you in the back, stole all your money, and ruined your life. It was awkward, not enticing.

After rehab I never really considered relapse as an option for me. There was something different this time that made it more serious. Again, that didn't make me immune, but there had been a clear shift in how I thought about recovery and sobriety.

It isn't because I am special; it's because I make a daily decision matched with daily surrender. It is doing the hard work, staying connected to God and community, and serving others that has kept me sober.

Relapse is very real, even if you've been sober for twenty years. Your guard must stay up, and your sobriety must stay protected. Every morning, and many times throughout your day, you must actively choose to stay connected and to choose recovery.

It's no simple task. Believe me.

chapter ten

Who Is Your Crew?

——— *Rob* ———

It was a real answer to prayer. With each passing month, we noticed Danielle's relational world getting broader and healthier. She had some genuine camaraderie with people in the recovery movement who were on the same journey as she was, but I also saw her expanding her circle of friends at church. It was good to see her connecting again with people in a more normal, everyday kind of way. It did my heart wonders to see her laughing and enjoying life again. A girls night out at the movies. A walk around town. And her favorite thing, hanging out at a coffee shop, having great conversations or reading a good book. I can't tell you how grateful I was that God was providing healthy, godly friends. They laughed together. They prayed and worshiped together. They shared authentically together. They were doing life together.

One of the things that haunted me the most about Danielle's addiction was how alone she was. I had no idea. I remember hopping in the car with Laura and Luke and driving eight hours north to celebrate Danielle's twentieth birthday. We took fifteen of her closest friends out to dinner at the Cheesecake Factory. We had great conversations with kids just like Danielle, who were pursuing their education, making memories, and dreaming big dreams. I was so happy for her. It was exactly what I wanted Danielle to experience at school, what Laura and I loved most from our own college days. Good friends and great memories. It seemed to me that Danielle was well-connected and well-liked. She had always been that way. But Danielle was only letting us see a small part of her life. The real story was devastatingly different.

As her addiction progressed, by her own choice, she became increasingly isolated. Day after day, our beautiful, vivacious, funny, life-giving daughter would stay in her room, skipping classes, watching Netflix, and secretly drinking. In a dorm surrounded by hundreds of people, she was utterly alone. I still get emotional when I think about it. She had everything going for her, but really, she had nothing. But that's the tragedy of addiction. What starts at a party with a room full of people often ends alone in a room all by yourself.

Jesus told a story about a young man who had everything. One day, the boy went up to his father and said, "Dad, I would like to go to college." So the father gave him his inheritance. (Okay, I'm taking a little creative license. But FYI, the cost of college nowadays equals an inheritance.) The boy got in his car and drove off to school, where he completely blew off the semester and wasted his life on alcohol, drugs, and parties. When the money ran out, the party friends disappeared. The alcohol dried up. The drugs flowed to the next foolish victim.

As fate would have it, there was a recession, and the only job he could find was on a local farm feeding the pigs. He was starving. His stomach was empty, but so was his heart. There was no more laughter. There were no more good times. There was no sense of pride and inner satisfaction at a job well done. There were no books or classes that were expanding his view of the world. There was no confirmation of the gifts and talents he was born with. He couldn't remember the last time he felt inspired by a song, a poem, a painting, or a story. Nothing moved him anymore. His ability to choose was shattered. His dreams were dead. His life was an endless loop of hopelessness. And the son found himself utterly and totally alone.

Jesus told the story of a prodigal son (Luke 15:11–32). We had a prodigal daughter . . .

— *Danielle* —

In my first year of sobriety, all the people I knew from rehab had relapsed. I don't want to lump them all together. They all had different stories. Some relapsed because of a broken heart, and others from the stress of parenting or work. The common thread? They had all disconnected from their community.

In rehab, community is guaranteed, but maintaining those connections outside of rehab isn't easy. I am not saying this is the only reason they relapsed; in fact, they probably dealt with things that made life seem impossibly hard. Not having support can make you feel all alone, and that's when it is the easiest to fall back into old habits. I knew all too well that tendency to isolate myself, which made me nervous about how important community was to my recovery.

I had no idea who my friends were, and I felt a little lost. My closest friends in recovery had relapsed, and I felt like I was starting new. Again. So as I started searching for new friendships, I thought the church would be a good place to start. However, I didn't quite know how to connect with people without drugs and alcohol or the common denominator of consuming massive amounts of those two things.

I was a little hesitant to dive into new friendships. Being a pastor's kid made it a little difficult for me to trust that people genuinely wanted to have a relationship with me. College was a little different; I was not Pastor Rob and Laura's daughter there. No one knew who I was. Meeting people happened a little bit more naturally in that environment because my guard was down. But now I was back in my parents' church, with a sincere desire to start fresh and build friendships, and I didn't know where to begin.

Now on top of being a pastor's kid, I was also a recovering alcoholic. So I had no idea if an authentic dynamic could exist in a friendship with all the things I brought to the table. Every night for a few weeks, I would go straight home after work and hang out with my parents. As awesome as they are, I felt so alone. Being alone reminded me of the darkness of my old life. That isolation of drinking alone in my dorm room was a painful memory I can never forget. I would spend days without leaving my bed. Being alone was fatal for me.

I had friends back then, but I didn't have a community, and there is a difference. I would be in a room full of bodies, but none of them were people to me. At first I got drunk with friends; that was fun. But over time, I noticed my drinking was different than theirs. Eventually nobody could keep up. So I decided if I was drinking alone with a group of people, I might as well drink alone without the people.

When I think back to my years in college and process that season of my life, I often find myself wondering if I should have picked a different crew. But every time I reminisce about those friends, I don't see awful people. The common denominator was that we were all searching. We were fresh in independence, trying to find life. The problem with my crew was that we were finding life in all the wrong places. There were students at my college finding life in the right places, but I didn't know them . . . I didn't *want* to know them.

My friends were fun. My friends skipped class with me in the middle of the day to escape and find the cheapest, most effective mimosas, which we drank out of gas station Big Gulp cups. We would drive to nowhere in particular, drink, laugh, and talk. In the beginning life didn't get much better than that. Even still, I feel a certain nostalgia about the less brutal memories. I thought I had found life. I thought I was free, happy, and independent. Just like the prodigal son, my friends and I were all searching for something but finding nothing.

I can honestly say that some of the people I surrounded myself with were bad news, but I can't blame anyone else for my actions. Most of my friends were decent people. They didn't know I was an addict. They weren't aware that the shot they were offering would activate my internal allergy. So I can't sit here and declare that my choice in friendships was the reason I spiraled out of control.

However, I do believe that your crew matters. I don't care who you are or how strong you think you are—every single person on this planet is influenced by others. So the question isn't, *Are you being influenced?* It's, *Who or what are you being influenced by?*

Looking back at my previous life, I find it hard to think about bad influences, because the truth of the matter is, out of all the bad influences I knew, I may have been the worst. In all honesty, I didn't know if I even had what it would take to be a good friend. I didn't know if I could care about other people's problems. I didn't know if I could listen to another person talk without drifting over to my own thoughts or agendas. I didn't just need to find a good community; I needed to learn how to be a part of one too.

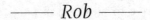

Rob

Because Danielle was in rehab over the holidays, she was not able to spend Christmas with the family. We decided to postpone our celebration until February. We left all the Christmas decorations up for two and a half months just so she could have a family Christmas. I'll never forget her sitting on the floor hugging her stocking, smiling from ear to ear. She was so grateful. We wanted her to know she would never lose the special place she had in our family. Relational connections are everything. It was a perfect celebration.

I think we instinctively knew that what Danielle needed more than anything else was the love and support of friends and family. I was completely convinced there was no way that Danielle would make it alone. She wasn't wired that way. I don't think anyone is. I heard somewhere that the only statistically verifiable common denominator in long-term sobriety is being a part of a group. Nobody makes it alone. Nobody! Not in recovery and not in life. Danielle would need healthy relationships for inspiration, encouragement, support, and companionship.

For Danielle to try to go it alone was unthinkable. I once watched a documentary on how lions prey on antelope. They look for the stragglers, those who have separated themselves from the herd, and then they attack. I knew that Danielle would be at her weakest if she ever separated herself from friends and family. Just like the straggling antelope, she would be vulnerable to an attack.

I was so gratified that Danielle was plugging in to church. I knew she would find some of the best friends in her life there. Friends who would pray with her. Friends who would hold her accountable. Friends who would create the safe space she needed and would help her acclimate to a healthy life. Other than Jesus himself, Danielle's friends had a more positive impact on her sobriety journey than anything else.

But that need for community wasn't just for Danielle. Laura and I relied heavily on our network of relationships as well. Right from the start, we decided we were not going to try to hide Danielle's issues. We told our friends. We were completely open and honest. When things were challenging, we asked them to pray with us, and they offered their encouragement and wisdom. When we celebrated a milestone, they celebrated with us. But most of all, they were just there. We drew strength from their strength, and it made all the difference in the world. I noticed an unexpected connection born out of our vulnerability. On my worst days, I would imagine people turning their backs on us because of our issues. But the truth was, our openness only drew us closer. Everyone needs friends and family because nobody makes it alone. Not addicts. And not those who love them.

The implications of the story of the prodigal son are both profound and far-reaching. When the young man made up his mind to return home, it set in motion a chain of events that has provided hope and inspiration to prodigals and their families in every generation. It brought hope to Danielle. It brought inspiration to me, especially the last few verses of the story. When the prodigal son returned home, the father loved him unconditionally and celebrated his return: "But the father said to his servants, 'Quick! Bring the best robe and put it on him. Put a ring on his finger and sandals on his feet. Bring the fattened calf and kill it. Let's have a feast and celebrate. For this son of mine was dead and is alive again; he was lost and is found.' So they began to celebrate" (Luke 15:22–24).

Being a parent of an addict was filled with challenges. It was not hard to understand why moms, dads, family, and friends would create distance from their troubled loved ones to protect their hearts from disappointment and pain. I felt it myself at times. Our ability to love was being tested. The story of the prodigal son set a whole new standard for me. It set the bar, and it flat-out inspired me. *God, help me be a father like you.* I saw in that story the kind of dad I wanted to be for Danielle. This story I had read countless times, and referenced at least once a year in my sermons, was now a road map for me.

The fact that the father in this story saw his son while he was "still a long way off" told me that the father was looking for him. Perhaps all day, every day. Maybe I should keep my hopes up.

The father was not filled with judgment, anger, humiliation, contempt, or frustration. He was filled with compassion. Maybe I should park my judgment elsewhere.

He ran to his son. It's the only time in the Bible that I saw God in a hurry. Wow! God runs to his kids when they're in trouble? That's stunning! Maybe I should always keep my running shoes nearby.

There were no reservations in the heart of the father. He wasn't holding back. He went all in, right away. He hugged him and kissed him. When the son began his rehearsed speech, the father interrupted him and restored him completely by putting a robe on his shoulders, sandals on his feet, and a ring on his finger. Maybe I should keep front and center the power of hugs and kisses.

(And on a side note, notice that the father said, "Bring the fattened calf and kill it." My wife, being a doctor, is always trying to get me to eat healthier. When she encourages me to eat more green beans, I remind her of this part in the story. The father didn't tell the servants to go steam some vegetables; he said go kill the fattened calf. The father wanted steak. I love that! And all the men said . . . *Amen!* I thought I would just throw that in.)

For Danielle, this story provided hope. God was looking for her. In the midst of Danielle's addiction, God was loving her. God ran to her. God threw his arms around her. God kissed her. God restored her. This story more than any other gave Danielle a glimpse into the heart of her heavenly Father. God was not angry, distant, disappointed, or vengeful. This story drove home the beauty of God's unconditional love for her. She knew she could always come home. And I believe that hope made all the difference.

The closing part of the story is not just a nice wrap-up, but rather it reveals one of the most important truths about lasting recovery. "And let us [invite everyone and] feast and celebrate" (Luke 15:23 AMP). The first thing the father did after he restored his son was throw a party, in part to celebrate the return of the son who had been lost. But the father also had a much more profound motivation. The father knew that if the son was going to stay, he would need the support of family and good friends. The son was in desperate need of some healthy relationships, so the father gave his son an opportunity to reconnect to his community, the people who would provide support and encouragement on his journey to wholeness. In telling about this gathering of friends and family, Jesus was saying that *nobody makes it alone.*

—— *Danielle* ——

It was uncomfortable for a little while. I had to put myself in situations that made my stomach tie up in knots. In my head, I am a really fun person, and alcohol seemed to make that fun person come out quickly. But life was different now. There was no quick fix. I had to actually put myself out there with no guarantee of acceptance. That is a scary thing to do, especially for a person who never thought she was good enough.

I went through a long process of trial and error. I met some interesting people, but none I felt a real heart connection to.

After some time, I felt a desire to start a volleyball group at my church. When I was in high school, I loved volleyball. I loved the thrill of competition and playing something I was pretty good at. So in an attempt to get in touch with the things that used to give me life, I went ahead and started the volley-ball group, even though I wasn't sure I knew how to lead it. I thought I was starting this volleyball hangout just to have a little fun . . . I had no idea what God had up his sleeve.

There was a girl from work, Sophie, whose office I passed by every day. Months went by, and we didn't have a single conversation. She and I are both shy, so it wasn't easy to spark small talk. Then slowly but surely, a few words were exchanged. We didn't talk much, but every time we did, it was so obvious we were destined to be friends. We were both awkward introverts looking for a community. Let me tell you, two introverts trying to form a friendship is truly a sight to see. There is no smooth way of asking an adult to be your friend. But since I had a volleyball group I could use as my cover, our friendship commenced.

It was an interesting progression because we went from barely talking to becoming best friends overnight. I craved friendship so badly that I poured out a million words that had been pent up from months of being alone. In Sophie I found the kindest, most generous, and most adventurous life-giving soul I have ever met. I do not deserve her friendship, but this isn't the first time God has given me more than I deserve.

Sophie and I encourage each other, listen intently, and call each other out on our crap. We are there for the highs and the lows. She is a real friend who taught me what a real friend is and how to be a real friend in return. She redeemed friendship for me. Sophie and I are now a part of a group of friends who love the Lord and encourage each other often.

Not every single person I initiated a friendship with stuck. But eventually, through willingness and vulnerability, I found the world's best group of friends. The crew I have today inspires me to be a better person. Their friendships make me stronger. Now I genuinely believe I could not live my old life. With my new friends, that kind of life just wouldn't be possible.

Still, to this day it's difficult to be fully vulnerable. But at some point, you have to decide to let yourself be fully known. You'll be surprised at how many of your most insane thoughts have been thought by another.

That is why your crew matters. Ask yourself who your friends are. Not because I want to throw any cliché lines about friendship at you. But speaking from experience, I know that having a good crew makes it very difficult to fall.

chapter eleven

I'm Sorry

—— *Rob* ——

We were on the verge of a huge milestone celebration. Danielle was approaching one year of sobriety. Every study ever done on recovery marks this date as a very significant accomplishment; the prospects of long-term recovery shift dramatically, with the chances of relapse going from very likely to somewhat unlikely. The meaning of this day was not lost on us, and we were all extremely proud of Danielle.

Over the course of the last twelve months, we had seen a profound transformation in Danielle's life. But Danielle was not the only one who was changing. We were changing too. Prior to Danielle we had no experience with recovery and addiction. We went into this battle as novices, but we were emerging on the other side with experience and some deeply held convictions. And those convictions were shaping how I pastored our church.

Over the course of the year, I became a champion for the recovery movement in our own fellowship, and I preached a six-week series on overcoming the hurts, habits, and hang-ups of life.

We also made the Celebrate Recovery program a huge priority. I visited the meetings from time to time, and I was always struck by its atmosphere of total acceptance and encouragement. These people were there for each other in ways I had not experienced before. There was humor. There was humility. And there was hope!

Even though Celebrate Recovery had been active in our church for years, I had the honor of leading the chip ceremony for the first time personally. I gave blue chips to those who wanted to start their journey. I was floored by the number of people who wanted a new beginning. It seemed like half the room was taking that brave initial step. I have always been aware at some level that the church is a hospital for the hurting, but I was surprised by the variety of issues that people were struggling with and the passion I sensed in them to be free. People from every walk of life were there.

But what impressed me even more was the boisterous support and cheers that were so freely and sincerely given. I could barely contain my emotions as I handed out red chips for those who were celebrating thirty days of sobriety. Green chips for those celebrating sixty days. White chips for ninety days. Yellow chips for six months. Black chips for nine months. There were gold coins to mark that magical one-year mark. Out of the gathering that night, five people came forward to receive that special chip.

I was proud of everyone who received a chip that night, but I was overwhelmingly grateful for the courageous accomplishment of my beloved daughter. For the first time in a long time, she had lived a year completely alcohol and drug free. There was a super loud applause when I called her name, and I felt very loved and supported, as though we had been adopted into a fraternity. These were my people.

I gave out a few more chips to those celebrating milestones of years and decades. It was a poignant reminder that the hard work of sobriety is a lifetime effort. I will never forget that night.

This mark in Danielle's journey brought lots of changes. Laura and I could tell that she was ready to move on from the sober living environment. After heart-to-heart talks and a check-in with our counselors, we all decided that the best option was for Danielle to move back home. She took over our upstairs guest room, and we were so thrilled to have her. We mutually agreed on some basic ground rules, and Danielle began the next chapter in her recovery.

One day, Danielle came home and told us she was ready to make a job change as well. Living at our home made the commute to the accounting office even longer. When a job as an assistant in the youth ministry area opened up at church, she jumped at the opportunity to apply. She was hired, and the entire staff was delighted to have her. As a part of her job, she also assisted with a Celebrate Recovery group for young people. She approached her work with enthusiasm and passion. It truly seemed like Danielle was on the right path.

— *Danielle* —

It was 6:03 a.m. My alarm hadn't even gone off yet, but I felt a sudden jolt of energy. Filled with excitement and genuine joy, I shot up out of my bed, said my morning prayers, and went over to my bathroom, where I noticed my reflection in the mirror. I was grinning from ear to ear.

I paused and stood there for a few moments, thinking, *Look how far this girl has come.* Then the positive self-talk moved from thought to reality. I began to speak out loud.

"You are strong. You are brave. You are an overcomer. You beat the odds. You deserve this. Wear that smile proudly today. Congratulations."

It was the truest moment of self-appreciation I had ever experienced.

It was my one-year anniversary of consecutive sobriety. I was more excited to celebrate this birthday than my actual birthday, which had been just a few months earlier. My family had plans to celebrate later that night, and I could hardly wait.

Of course we had already celebrated many smaller milestones in the recovery journey up to this point, but at first it was difficult for me to celebrate. I felt like I didn't deserve a cookie just for no longer destroying my life. But that wasn't true. I *did* deserve to be celebrated. I needed to give myself grace. I had owned up to my past, and it was 100 percent necessary to commemorate the positive changes I had made in my life.

The truth is that I should be celebrating my recovery every day. If you knew me in my old life, then you know it is only by a miracle from the Lord that I'm sitting here still breathing. That is something to jump up and down and shout about.

Celebrate your victories. Life will be much more fun that way.

With this huge milestone behind me, I began to feel the need for something new. I was so grateful for the healing that took place at inpatient treatment and then outpatient treatment and sober living, but I knew I was entering a new season in my recovery. That didn't come stress free. I absolutely had fears. Sober living was a safe place with good people, but having a year of sobriety under my belt and a reliable support system to return to, I felt the release to make the change.

One week after my one-year sobriety anniversary, I packed up all my things and made the bittersweet transition to my parents' house. I was also ready to make a career change. There was a job available at our church for someone to lead a ministry for young people in recovery, so I transitioned from the accounting firm to my new position at the church.

—— *Rob* ——

Looking back on the first year, I could see the importance of honest communication and active forgiveness. So much of Danielle's addiction season was filled with lies, half-truths, and manipulations, and now that she was on the road to recovery, she wanted to express sincere apologies. It was the right and healthy thing to do. She needed to say she was sorry, and she needed to hear that she was forgiven. During the first year of Danielle's recovery, there were lots of apologies. Some of the issues were obvious. But others were deeper and subtler. Like the peeling of an onion, each layer on the road to healing exposed another layer.

The forgiveness dynamic started in earnest during Family Week when Danielle was in rehab. There was a powerful moment in front of the whole group when Danielle asked us for forgiveness for specific things she did. Forgiveness for lying, for wasting college tuition money, for not heeding our advice, and so on. As the year unfolded and Danielle became more aware, there were deeper levels of heartfelt connection and reconciliation. She apologized for the sleepless nights. For ruining vacations. For all of the stress and worry and anxiety she caused. For putting her life at risk on the same road where we had already lost a son. For missing Thanksgivings, Christmases, and birthdays. Each apology was like a healing balm to us. Just hearing the confessions and saying in response, "You are forgiven," made a huge difference. Nothing would change our love for Danielle; however, knowing that she was aware of the pain and heartache she had caused was truly life-giving. There is something beautifully supernatural in hearing a sincere apology and then extending heartfelt forgiveness.

For Danielle to have those specific offenses covered in compassion was life-transforming as well. It's a huge burden to live with guilt and shame. When she experienced the full grace of forgiveness, you could see the weight lifting off her shoulders. It brought us closer than we've ever been before. It is not surprising that the core of Christianity is *forgiveness*.

Danielle was not the only one who needed to ask for forgiveness, however. I also had to own my mistakes. I had to apologize for overreacting. I had to ask for forgiveness for enabling. In one of the more tender moments of this reconciliation process, I asked Danielle to forgive me for being so consumed with my own grief that I was not as sensitive as I needed to be to what the loss of her brother had done to *her*. I asked her forgiveness for not seeing what I should've seen even years later when she was in college. It's good to say you're sorry. And it's beautiful to hear that you are forgiven.

We noticed, however, that what flowed naturally and authentically in our relationship with Danielle was not replicated in all the families we observed. Sometimes the relational wreckage was so extensive that family members didn't have the emotional capacity to extend that grace. It was heartbreaking. But to be honest, it wasn't always easy for me to forgive. To have to fight another intense battle so soon after losing our son was brutal. But whenever I felt tempted to hold on to an offense, I tried to think about what Jesus did for me. He forgave every sin every time. And he encouraged us to forgive others just as he had forgiven us. Not once. Not twice. Not even seven times. But seventy times seven. In other words, we need to keep on forgiving, no matter what.

—— *Danielle* ——

Making amends is the heartbeat of recovery.

In the Twelve-Step program, steps eight and nine ask us to

consider our entire lives and list any and all people who have harmed us or whom we have harmed. After we've made our list, we are then to make amends with them all.

For most people, this may be the most difficult task of them all. To list all the people who have harmed you or whom you have harmed often means rehashing very painful memories, when most of the time you want these memories to stay in the past. Resentment stops you from allowing full healing to take place. I think it's hard for people to forgive because the pain has become a part of them, and forgiveness means losing that. As twisted as it sounds, pain can be comforting, because at least it's familiar. But this unhealed pain leaves only two options: relapse or restoration.

If long-term recovery is something you want, then your only option is to face your past.

As expected, this was the most heart-wrenching and difficult process of recovery to walk through. I didn't realize how many hurts I was hanging on to. I remembered a wide variety of hurts, from getting in trouble in my second-grade classroom to feeling devastated about losing the closest person to me. I had a lot of wounds and a lot of unforgiveness. I didn't know how to handle the scar of losing Caleb. I was mad at him, but I didn't want to admit it. It felt wrong to speak or think anything negative about him. But the truth was, I was mad. I was mad at him for leaving. I was mad that he chose to drive that late at night. I was mad at God for letting it happen. I was mad that I couldn't tell him in person how mad I was.

Something interesting happened when I finally found the

courage to express my anger out loud. I discovered I wasn't alone; many other people felt similar emotions toward their loved ones. Expressing my anger wasn't easy, and it didn't produce immediate forgiveness, but it started the journey.

Growing up in the church, I was embarrassed to share the deep, dark emotions I had. I was never specifically told to keep them in, but I felt like there had to be a limit, especially as a pastor's kid. I felt my deepest and darkest parts should stay in, but I could let my surface-level, "easily fixable" issues show. You will never get healing if you never acknowledge the things you need healing from. It's important to verbalize the things that have hurt you, even if it feels scary and wrong to admit them.

The only thing harder than remembering all the pain that people have caused you is remembering all the pain you have caused people. For addicts, remembering the hurts you have caused others is a slow burn. Although painful, it's much easier for us to remember and feel the pain inflicted on us. It is not in our nature to really internalize and process how we've treated others. Don't get me wrong, it's not difficult for us to remember a time we mistreated someone, because that is rather obvious. In fact, by the time we decide to get sober, we've usually created a large wake of relational wreckage behind us. We may be aware of that wreckage, but it takes the process of returning to our humanity to actually care enough to apologize from our hearts.

Some of the damage we create is too big to fix with a simple apology, even if it's heartfelt. Most of this damage exists for the ones we love the most, which can be the most painful to accept. We hurt them because we assumed there was nothing we could do that would make them stop loving us. We took advantage of them, lied to their faces, stole their money, broke their trust, and manipulated and used them. This type of damage requires what we call a living amends.

A living amends is an apology through your actions over a long period of time.

A living amends is an apology through your actions over a long period of time. The only way you can prove the authenticity of your apology is for your sobriety to be verified over and over again. You may need to say you are sorry as many times as someone needs to hear it. But the real amends is you living out your healthy life, sane and sober.

chapter twelve

Pay It Forward

— *Danielle* —

I love the movie *Pay It Forward*. In it, a middle school social studies teacher challenges her students to think of an idea that can change the world and then do it. With childlike excitement, one of the students decides to start a chain of kindness. He begins the project by finding three people for whom he can do a random act of kindness. They in return are to find three new people to pay the favor forward. In the movie, the ripple effects of this student's kindness reach farther than he could have ever imagined.

In recovery there is a similar approach to giving back commonly referred to as sponsorship. You choose someone to take you through your Twelve-Step recovery journey, and then you take that experience and walk someone new through their recovery journey. Sponsoring someone opens our eyes to see that we, even though we are recovering addicts, can show kindness. That we can overcome our innate selfish tendencies and reach out to help another. Fellow addicts know exactly what I mean when I say it's baffling at first to find that helping others also helps us. Yet we find that in our service to others, God restores us to sanity.

My sponsoring season looked a little different. Instead of meeting with someone one-on-one, I led a Celebrate Recovery group for youth. Only being a year sober, I was initially worried that it was too early to take on a role where I was in charge of helping others. Maybe I needed to become more seasoned in this recovery game for a little while longer. Honestly, my selfish side wanted the focus to stay on me and my needs. I had a lot of fear about taking on this new role, but sometimes you just need to do it afraid. And I'm so glad I did, because I got to see some amazing transformations.

For example, a girl who was very shy came to the class. She would come and go without saying anything. You could tell just by looking in her eyes that she had a story to tell, but I knew it needed to unfold in her time. One day after the class ended and everyone had left, she asked in a timid, cracked voice if she could talk to me. I sat down with her, and she began to tell me all the harsh realities of her childhood, which led to her insecurities, which led to her filling that void with sleeping around. At school every day, kids would call her a slut, and she felt like she had no choice but to wear that label. The only thing that could numb the pain was alcohol and more guys. She dated boys who treated her poorly because she didn't know what else to do. She felt like the only real chance of escape was death. This broke my heart.

I began to pray over her silently as I looked intently into her eyes and said, "It doesn't matter what mistakes you've made.

You are *not* what people say you are. You are worthy." I knew in that moment my words would only go so far, so I kept it short. Sometimes giving a whole sermon is not what someone needs. All she needed to know was that I was there, that I heard everything she said and still thought she was worthy. That's all. My own experiences helped me know how to handle that situation, even though her family background was different from mine.

Over the next couple of weeks, she returned, and each time she shared and opened up a little more. Then her sharing turned from sad stories to small victories, and then from small victories to big victories. She broke things off with her verbally abusive boyfriend. She stopped sleeping around. And she started dreaming about what her life could be because she no longer had the chains holding her back from a better reality. She was free—and wearing that freedom so well.

There are many heartbreaking, miraculous healing stories like hers, and I'm so grateful that I get to watch them unfold right before my eyes. I was amazed at what God was capable of doing through me. A disobedient, impure addict like me. He takes our wounds and heals them, but he doesn't stop there. He uses them to bring healing to others. I couldn't believe this was my story, and now it was hers too.

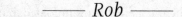 *Rob*

I had always been more reserved than vulnerable and open. In fact, the first two years of married life for Laura and me were more difficult than they should've been because of this issue. Laura was the opposite. She was open and free about everything. There wasn't a story she couldn't tell or an experience that was off-limits. People loved her for it. She was real. She was honest. She told it like it was. They could relate to her vulnerability. I, on the other hand, liked to shape the stories. To my way of thinking, it was only appropriate to be vulnerable when it put you in the best light. It was okay to be vulnerable about innocent mistakes or funny quirks. But it was inappropriate to share about personal weakness, bad choices, or things that might alter the carefully scripted picture of a man and his family who had their act together. I wanted to be the one with all the answers. I wanted to project strength. I was more interested in presenting the image that everything was good and great in our world. No weaknesses. No chinks in the armor. Our marriage was fantastic. Our church was growing. Our kids were healthy. Life was good. Period.

Sometimes this weakness of mine played out in big ways, and sometimes it manifested in semantics. We laugh at it now. Laura would say, "Rob and I had a big fight this week." Once the cat was out of the bag, I would rephrase it. "We didn't have a big fight; we had an elevated discussion." "I didn't eat the whole bag of cookies; I had a few on a special occasion." "I didn't forget to take the trash out; I was spending time in prayer." Yeah, right. Any personal struggles or real issues were minimized. I got better at being authentic as the years unfolded, but posing was still my default posture. I was the same way when it came to talking about Danielle's addiction. "Danielle wasn't an addict; she was just having a college experience."

In the summer after Danielle finished rehab, I was talking with our creative team at Shoreline about the possibility of doing a series of three sermons on the topic of recovery. One of the team members suggested that Danielle could tell her story by video in five-minute clips each Sunday. When Danielle heard about the possibility, she was all in. I, however, had deep reservations. It's one thing to be open with close friends and family, but another thing entirely to be open with everyone in our church. I didn't want Danielle to live with the stigma of being an addict. I also have a tendency toward privacy, and frankly, her story didn't match my cherished script of a pastor's family that has it all together. But Danielle was adamant. It was her story and she wanted to share it. Reluctantly, I gave in.

The sermon series was very well received, and the response to Danielle's story was overwhelming. Many people were freed to deal with their own issues because we were being so honest and real about ours. The recovery ministry in our church saw a huge increase in involvement. And Danielle's video clips on Facebook and on our website were the most watched and shared video clips our church has ever produced.

This experience taught me that authentic vulnerability opens the door to people's hearts and paves the way for real human connectedness. Like many people, I felt the pressure to act like I had it all together. But the truth was, I didn't. I had issues; our family had issues; and our daughter had issues. When we shared from the heart about our struggles, something truly amazing happened. Instead of diminishing our influence and undercutting our leadership as I feared it would, it enhanced both.

The truth is, nobody relates to perfection. We are all human. And I've never met a human who hasn't failed. And I have never met a human who has it all together. So why should I continue the charade? The more open and honest I was, the more people leaned in. The more vulnerable I was, the more open they were about their own challenges. And it gave us the opportunity to do something we longed to do—help people with our story.

One of the most heartwarming experiences in our recovery journey was how much help we received from others in the movement. In fact, helping others is part of the DNA of recovery. You give back. Almost all the professionally trained counselors who really helped Danielle navigate through the flawed think-ing that fueled her addiction had a recovery story themselves. I was so grateful that they courageously turned their personal battle into a mission to set others free. Their freedom helped bring us freedom.

I will never forget the weekly phone calls when Danielle's counselors would update us on her progress in rehab. They were not only counseling Danielle; they were counseling us. They often had the perfect words to calm our fears and give us perspective. And what about the volunteers in the recovery movement? They are the real heroes. I was amazed at the selfless sacrifice and heartfelt determination that guided their efforts. They took their own recovery seri-ously and were passionate about helping others as well. They knew all the tricks and were well-acquainted with all the lies and manipulations. They had been there and done that.

They knew exactly how to deal with Danielle because they had walked in her shoes.

People in our lives stepped up in unexpected ways too. One of the wives we had met when I coached Luke's and Caleb's baseball team volunteered to be a sponsor for Danielle. She was a godsend. Laura and I had no idea that she had her own battle with alcohol and was actively involved in Celebrate Recovery at her church. She was perfect for Danielle. Her wisdom and faith gave Danielle—and us—hope.

I remember sitting outside a church one night that had opened its doors to a Twelve-Step program that Danielle was involved in. As I waited to drive her home, I was filled with gratitude for that church and what it was doing for our daughter, and I resolved that night that we were going to do whatever we could to support the recovery movement in our own church. We had been helped, and I wanted to give back.

Last year, we were blessed to host the very first national convention for Celebrate Recovery at Shoreline. Thousands of people from all over the country came to learn and celebrate their freedom. Our entire family had been impacted by hundreds of volunteers. We were the beneficiaries of the "pay it forward" mentality that is so beautifully ingrained in recovery, and now we wanted to add our church's strength to the movement.

Opportunities to give back pop up all the time, and they are so vital for both the addict and an addict's family during recovery. Helping others like you have been helped is in the DNA of recovery, and it's a beautiful embodiment of Christ's love for us.

— *Danielle* —

During my recovery journey, I was completely unaware of the impact I could have, even in treatment. The program I attended was led by a man and a woman who had successfully walked through their own recovery journeys. They both meant a lot to me, but I had a particular connection to Jack, the male leader. He was born and raised Catholic, so I felt like he understood to some degree my desire to have a relationship with Jesus. I would often share in our groups about how much I loved church. I got the impression that he had not experienced church the way I had, but he listened and validated my desire to reconnect to my Higher Power.

Being the little evangelist I was, I would often come to my group stocked with invites for any special events coming up at church. A few weeks before Easter, I brought invitations to our Easter service and handed them out to the whole group, even though I had no expectation that anyone would attend.

Fast-forward one month to the last day of my outpatient treatment program. On your last day, a mini-ceremony called a commencement is held where everyone goes around the room and gives the person graduating a constructive criticism and tells them something they are proud of. Jack went first. With tears in his eyes, he told me that recently in his life, things had been really tough—so tough that he was feeling completely hopeless. For the first time in his recovery, he realized he spiritually needed something more, something real.

There is no recovery goal you need to meet before you can start helping people.

On Easter morning he was at the end of his rope. He needed a God experience. Racking his brain on where to go to get this thing his soul was craving, he remembered the Catholic church he attended growing up, and he went to their early service. There he waited for a divine connection that just didn't come. He went home feeling even more hopeless than before. As he sat down to cry, he knocked over his teaching book from our class—and out popped the invite to Shoreline's Easter service. A spark of hope ignited. Seeing that the service started at 11:00 a.m., he glanced at his clock to find he could make it if he hurried. So he jumped up immediately and drove to Shoreline.

That day at my commencement ceremony, he tilted his head up and looked straight at me as he concluded the story. "That service changed my life, Danielle. Any impact I have had on you these last couple months pales in comparison to what you have done for me." Tears rolled down his cheek. "I just needed you to know that."

This was almost four years ago. Jack is still an active member of Shoreline today.

Jack had no idea the impact he had on my life. I learned so much from his leadership in recovery, but I never expected *my* life could also have an impact on *him*. There is no recovery goal you need to meet before you can start helping people. In fact, waking up this morning is all the permission you need to be a helping hand.

Don't limit yourself to a fixed way you can give back. Don't put a cap on the people you can reach. You don't need to be fixed up and polished; that doesn't even exist anyway. God is the one who is orchestrating this. When he gives you an opportunity in life to make a difference and do his work, it just isn't about you anymore.

So pay it forward.

chapter thirteen

Living Free

—— *Rob* ——

My car was packed with all of Danielle's stuff. She was moving again. For the last seventeen months she had been living in our upstairs guest room, and it had been an absolute delight to have her. Seeing our daughter blossom into a mature, carefree, fun-loving, compassionate adult was a constant source of joy. It seemed like every day the deep, dark claws of addiction receded to where it was difficult to even imagine where she was just a few years ago. We were extremely grateful! She had collected her two-year sobriety chip. As a family we celebrated two sober Thanksgivings and Christmases together, and two substance-free New Year's Eve parties.

Over that time, Danielle worked hard in her responsibilities at church. She had a real connection with the young people in youth ministry. They loved her realness and sense of humor.

She helped lots of kids through "The Landing," Shoreline's ministry for kids wrestling with addiction or living in families where addictions were causing dysfunction. She was making a real difference with her life.

She had found a healthy rhythm. While working full-time, she decided to go back to school. She continued her education online, pursuing a degree in leadership with an emphasis on ministry. She expanded her friendships. She now had a circle of girls in her life that Laura and I had always hoped she'd find. They were healthy, solid, fun-loving, caring, and adventurous, and it was obvious that their company gave Danielle life.

Danielle was also discovering activities she enjoyed. She pursued hiking and rock climbing, poetry, and good books. And, of course, coffee shops with friends. It was so good just to see Danielle enjoy life again.

Danielle moved into an apartment with one of her friends, signing a year lease. She was now responsible for her own rent, utilities, food, and entertainment. It was the next step in recovery—Danielle taking full responsibility for her life and choices. Laura and I were aware that any change could poten-tially bring new triggers, so we covered her with our prayers, kept a watchful eye, and trusted the Lord to keep her safe.

With Danielle on her own, we wondered if she would still want to be a part of our Monday family night. For as long as I can remember, we had a designated night where we would share a meal together, play a game, talk about the highlights of the week, and pray together. She put our hearts at ease. With a smile she told us that family night was nonnegotiable. I was so grateful that she loved it as much as we did.

Things were going so well that it was easy to forget that Danielle had almost destroyed her life with alcohol. Her counselors made a convincing case that she had a disease, and I remembered Danielle saying, "To drink is to die," but it was hard for me to reconcile the danger that alcohol still presented with the confident girl happily packing her stuff to move on to the next adventure in life. I wanted to make sure we weren't being overconfident.

I've always been a "lists" guy. Lists of things to do. Lists of daily confessions. Packing lists. Lists of daily routines. I thought it would be a good idea to make a list of the critical things that Laura and I had learned, so we could focus on maintaining Danielle's sobriety and our joy. So here is our list of lessons learned in recovery—lessons we still live out every day.

1. We must focus on victory one day at a time. One of the biggest challenges Laura and I faced when Danielle started her recovery was the daunting thought that she had to stay sober for the rest of her life. Danielle didn't know how that would be possible, and we had serious doubts ourselves. Drinking and drug abuse had become such an ingrained part of her daily experience that it was hard to imagine her life without it. She wanted to live free for the rest of her life, but she didn't think she could.

Laura and I finally realized we didn't have to approach Danielle's sobriety as a commitment for the rest of our lives. Instead, we had to approach it *one day at a time.* We didn't have to think about freedom for the rest of her life; we just had to think about her living free for one day. After that one day of freedom, we would do it again. Living free one day at a time was much more doable. Focus on victory one day at a time.

As parents, we also had to focus on and celebrate each day's victory. We had to manage our own emotions one day at a time. We had to live by faith one day at a time. We had to be grateful for each day of sobriety. Jesus seems to think that focusing on one day at a time is a good idea as well, because he taught us to pray, "Give us today our daily bread" (Matthew 6:11). Notice he didn't teach us to pray, "Give us this month our monthly bread." I tended to ask God to change me and Danielle forever, but he whispered back, "I'll change you today. I'll give you what you need for victory today."

After all, Danielle didn't get into the mess she was in over-night. It took months and years for this addiction to attach a vise-grip hold on her life, and she wasn't going to be fixed in a week or two. Even when she received her two-year sobriety chip, it wasn't the time for anyone to relax. Victory one day at a time is a commitment for life.

2. *We must live in the moment.* If focusing on victory one day at a time is the first step, then living in the moment in each day is the second. It was really easy for me to live each day with an undercurrent of anxiety, and it was having a huge negative impact on my life. Anxiety is a subtly destructive force. I found myself splitting my energy between past mistakes and future problems, thus sabotaging my ability to live life well. Focusing on regrets from the past is something that was and continues

to be a huge struggle for me. There are times when I am over-whelmed by the desire to go back and change our story, but I can't live in the past. Instead, I need to do what the apostle Paul advised, and forget what is behind me (Philippians 3:13).

Of course, living focused solely on the future doesn't help either. When part of my energy was preoccupied with the regrets and failures of yesterday and another part was con-sumed with the concerns of tomorrow, there was no energy left for me to live in the moment. And victory is always found by living in the moment. I found comfort in Jesus' words: "Give your entire attention to what God is doing right now, and don't get worked up about what may or may not happen tomorrow. God will help you deal with whatever hard things come up when the time comes" (Matthew 6:34 MSG).

I felt the Holy Spirit whisper, "Don't focus on past mistakes, and don't focus on future worries; live in the present." I knew that living preoccupied with my past mistakes or worrying about Danielle's future would never give me the energy I'd need to be of help to anyone. I couldn't afford my energy being depleted by regrets, worries, fears, and what-ifs. I had to focus on liv-ing in the moment.

I felt the Holy Spirit whisper, "Don't focus on past mistakes, and don't focus on future worries; live in the present."

3. *We must check our emotional tank frequently.* Danielle's recovery was not a sprint; it is a marathon—a day-after-day, month-after-month, year-after-year grind. Many times Laura and I didn't fully comprehend the emotional toll of the recovery process. We would feel exhausted and tired, and at

times we became easily frustrated. Small everyday annoyances that we could normally easily absorb became much more taxing. Finally, over time, we learned we had to check the gauge on our emotional tank. Just as we need to check the gas gauge to know the level of fuel in a vehicle, we also had to check our emotional gauge to make sure we weren't getting dangerously low.

We wanted to live aware so we could take corrective action to "fill up" our emotional tanks. After all, if we didn't take care of ourselves, how could we possibly help Danielle? So Laura and I began to check in with each other daily, each asking how the other was feeling and what the gauge on their emotional tank was telling them. If either one of us was low, we would find things to do to replenish our emotional reserves. We would engage in a fun activity we both enjoyed, or on some rare occasions we'd get away for an extra day or two. Laura and I wanted to make sure that when Danielle needed to fill her tank, we had some fuel to give.

4. *We must rely on God's power.* For us to live with peace and joy and provide the support and encouragement that Danielle needed, it required a nonnegotiable reliance on God's power. To connect ourselves to that power, we took time to pray, connected to our life-giving local church, trusted and relied on the promises in God's Word, and received refreshment from seeking out God's presence. If willpower had been all we needed, Laura and I would've never wrestled with all our doubts and fears. There were many times I felt powerless to do anything about the circumstances that were destroying my family, and I needed God's help. We learned to treasure the promise of

Philippians 4:13: "I can do everything through Christ, who gives me strength" (NLT).

5. We must focus on doing good, not feeling good. Laura and I realized what everyone eventually does—nobody gets to where they want to be on feelings alone. If you wait until you *feel* like changing, you never will. Most people have heard some version of this truth: it's always easier to act your way into a feeling than to feel your way into an action. Let's face it, at the beginning no addict ever "feels" like changing.

Danielle had to focus on doing good and let the feelings catch up later, and we as parents had to do the same thing. Many times, we didn't feel up to the challenge. Many times, we felt discouraged, and more than just a few times we felt a lot of self-pity.

Sometimes Laura and I had to do the right thing, even when we didn't feel like it. We would get up. Have our quiet time. Work out. Go to work. We had to do what we knew we had to do until the feelings caught up. I've learned that my feelings would eventually respond to the decisions and actions I took. Sometimes I didn't feel like having tough conversations, holding Danielle accountable, staying positive, or taking days off to meet with counselors. But I had to focus on doing good and not worry about the feelings. Feelings follow actions, not the other way around.

6. We must demonstrate our love in healthy ways. One of my biggest challenges with Danielle was my tendency to help her in ways that were counterproductive and ultimately unhealthy. I had to learn to set boundaries and not let my own insecurities dictate how I interacted with her. I had to make sure I wasn't enabling her bad behavior, and I had to stop fixing her problems and bailing her out of her difficult circumstances. I learned there was a difference between healthy and unhealthy love. Sometimes the most loving thing I could do was pray and let her figure it out for herself. And when I felt like she was on the right track, I needed to offer her all the encouragement I could.

For as long as I could remember, I was too quick to solve the problems Danielle created for herself. Sometimes the most loving thing to do is to *not* do something. Let circumstances teach their own life lessons. It has been my experience that addicts are unusually gifted at manipulation and pulling on the heartstrings. If you combine that with all regrets and hidden guilt that parents naturally already feel for "not being perfect," it's easy to see how unhealthy love practices develop. There is a desire in every family to help each other. It's what families do. But I wanted to make sure that the help I was so passionate about giving would actually help Danielle be truly free.

Romans 8:28 declares, "We know that in all things God works for the good of those who love him." That promise was absolutely fulfilled throughout this journey. Danielle and I are closer than we've ever been. God is using our story to touch and inspire thousands of people in our own community and beyond. And Laura and I are so blessed and grateful for the incredible family we have and the redemption we have experienced. God is the God of freedom. And if he did it for us, he can do it for anyone.

chapter fourteen

The Serenity Prayer

— *Danielle* —

It was packing day. I was lying on my bed and staring at the ceiling, watching the fan go around and around as my mind did the same. With conflicting emotions, I considered the fear of launching out on my own and the excitement of something new. I sat there reminiscing on the last couple of years. I remembered where I had been, crippled by addiction, and how far God had brought me. That gave me hope.

I lived at my parents' house for seventeen months after sober living. In my first two years of sobriety, these living situations were my safe places. Having a safe place is not a bad thing; in fact, in the beginning it's crucial to your recovery to be surrounded by a nonthreatening environment. It is also equally crucial to your recovery to keep moving forward. Eventually you have to take the risk and jump into a new season.

My life was falling into place. As I sat and looked at my future, it was abundantly clear to me that God's grace had been so beautifully threaded into my whole journey. His grace kept me alive as I guzzled down vodka shots and drove home drunk. His grace reached into my darkest season and pulled me into the light. His grace walked me through my first few years in sobriety, and his grace was delivering me to this new season of independence. His grace has met me at every turn.

It was time to move out of my parents' house and gain some independence. I had recently developed a friendship with a girl named Krysta, who started working at the church just a few months after me. We were in similar seasons in our lives, and by similar seasons, I mean *single*. We got along well. We hadn't known each other too long before moving in together, but we knew enough to give it a shot.

In the spring of 2017, as a twenty-two-year-old woman with two years of sobriety under my belt, I officially entered adulthood.

Krysta remained my roommate for a little less than three years. We lived together for a year in an apartment, and then in April 2018, we moved into a house. We've even added two more roommates into the mix. The memories made in this house are unmatched. I have never enjoyed life more. The group of girls I live with are the cream of the crop. We stay up many nights laughing until we cry and sharing the deepest parts of our souls. I have the best friendships on the planet, and I'm constantly surprised at what good friends they are to me. I aim to be that surprising in return.

I now work in women's ministry as a project manager, and I still lead Celebrate Recovery for youth. I love what I do, and I can't believe I get to do it.

I continue to make my recovery a priority and surrender to God daily. I stay aware of my condition and never graduate from self-help. I see my sponsor a couple of times a month. I'm always looking for opportunities to grow.

Today I am an honest, functioning member of my family and am still actively pursuing my living amends to them. I strive to earn back their trust a little more each day.

For the first two and a half years of sobriety, I chose not to date, both because recovery had a one-year no-dating rule and because I'd had dysfunctional relationships in the past. I was cautious and didn't want to rush into anything.

However . . .

In the spring of 2016, I met a boy—an amazing man who loves the Lord with all of his heart and treats me better than I deserve. He is more than I ever could have imagined for myself, and on July 19, 2019, I became his wife. Honestly, I didn't know if a healthy relationship could even be in the cards for me, but God knew.

I never thought this type of life could be possible for me. I broke the trust of the people I love. I destroyed my body without a second thought. I gave myself to people who are not my husband. I lied like it was my second language. And I used people to get what I wanted.

I do not deserve the life I have today.

But grace found me.

My past does not define me anymore; grace does. I need you to know that if this life of freedom is possible for me, then it is absolutely possible for you. And if you are a loved one of an addict, their recovery is possible, and they need you to believe in them.

The Serenity Prayer is a powerful statement that is recited in many recovery meetings, Christian and secular alike. The prayer sums up the entirety of recovery, and modeling life after these words is one of the only reasons I'm still sober today. To say them is one thing. To believe them is another. And to actually do them is the whole point.

Based on the Serenity Prayer, I share with you my mind-set and the lifestyle I pursue in order to stay free:

1. *God, grant me the serenity to accept the things I cannot change.* A behavior common to an addict like me is to believe I have the power to run the show. In my life, many things happened to me that were outside my control, so I hesitated to relinquish any bits of control I thought I had. The problem with this mind-set is that I forgot that the only one who has the power to orchestrate my life is God. So I stubbornly fought the inevitable, wasting my energy in an attempt to control what happened to me. But even with my best efforts, my life was unsuccessful.

After many attempts to quit drinking or to better myself, I eventually realized I didn't have the power at all. Nothing I tried worked, so I eventually came to the end of myself. Instead, I had to turn to the one who was in control—God—and learn to trust him and let him take the reins in my life. Now, to maintain long-term recovery, I have to surrender to God's plan every single day, if not many times a day, and I have to ask God daily to give me the grace to submit to his will. If I don't do that, I am sure to relapse.

2. *Courage to change the things I can.* I always wanted to change the things that I couldn't, and I never wanted to choose to change the things I could. Power to change comes from God, but the willingness comes from you. In a moment of temptation, I must be willing to ask God for the courage to say no while also acknowledging that the ability to say no does not come from me. If I had the power to say no, I would have saved myself from a lot of years of destruction. Humility is absolutely *key* in being able to change the things that you can. Because the moment I decide it is *my* power that made this change possible, I have immediately taken back control.

Pride is a one-way ticket to relapse.

I must be humbly willing to ask God for the courage to say no, because pride is a one-way ticket to relapse.

3. *And wisdom to know the difference.* I have to always remember that my mind is capable of manipulation, even of myself. I can convince myself of anything if I want it bad enough. Maintaining a strong connection with God and asking for his divine guidance diminish my chances of making a decision that's outside his will. If I am not connected to God and I want something that isn't good for me, I know I will enter a dangerous spot. It may start with something small, but give it a few weeks, and I'll be convincing myself that I have changed enough to drink again.

4. *Living one day at a time, enjoying one moment at a time.* Every morning when I wake up, I sit straight up in my bed and do something called four-count breathing. This essentially is a

method of breathing that gives you a moment to consider where you are and what you're doing. I spent so many years blurring and escaping my reality that I never wanted to do that again. Life, no matter how you spin it, will never be perfect. But that's the beauty of living one day and one moment at a time. Living this way immediately takes me out of selfish living. Living in the moment requires *being present* in the moment, which requires listening and experiencing.

This concept also reminds me that there are more moments than the one I am currently in. To me that means that when temptation strikes, I can play the tapes through and know that a few moments from now, I will be grateful I didn't stop to buy that drink. You are only as sober as you are in the moment in front of you.

5. *Accepting hardship as a pathway to peace.* This concept is still the hardest one for me to accept. I have spent a large portion of my life avoiding pain, yet my only promise of peace is to go *through* hardships. This may be the most important piece of this prayer, because in one sentence, it exposes my fear of pain, while at the same time it commands me to accept my hardships as the only real path to freedom. I have no choice but to face pain and hardships and deal with them, no matter how hard it is or how uncomfortable it feels.

This was an intimidating request for me. But I knew that if I returned to a life of alcohol and drugs, I would never break through to that promise of peace. Now I force myself to feel and pursue peace with my whole heart, no matter how hard that process is. The alternative is just not worth it to me.

6. *Taking, as Jesus did, this sinful world as it is, not as I would have it.* It's difficult sometimes to realize that the goal is to be sober for the rest of my life. I need to understand how sinful the world can be and how vulnerable I am to its fleeting satisfactions so that I know how to guard my life. The opportunities to sin will never go away. Therefore I can no longer be in the world the way I used to, with no intentionality.

That's why giving back and sharing your journey with another person is so important. Giving back is the perfect example of being in the world but not of it.

6. *Trusting that You will make all things right if I surrender to Your will.* Recovery is a process. There are no shortcuts. There is no GPS with an estimated time of arrival. In fact, there is no arrival at all. The process of recovery unfolds over a lifetime. Yet it's not hard for me to believe that God has the ability to make all things right.

However, it is hard for me to trust that it will happen as soon as I want it to. The other part is fear. What if his plans clash with mine? What if I don't want what he has for me?

But the truth is, none of my plans have ever worked. God knows me better than I know myself. I have to remind myself that this fear is a lie. If I need proof, I can look at the track record . . .

Score:
> God: bajillion
> Danielle: 0

7. So that I may be reasonably happy in this life and supremely happy with You forever in the next. Amen. It somehow takes the pressure off when I remember that this life is not the end goal. God put us here for a reason, and life is meant to be enjoyed and lived to the fullest, but it is not the whole point. God is.

I used to get discouraged when I read this last part of the Serenity Prayer. I would think, *I want to be more than just reasonably happy.* But then I realized that being supremely happy by human standards can only be reasonably happy compared to heavenly standards.

If you get anything from reading this book, I hope it is that you are not alone. If God can do this for me, he can most certainly do it for you. The truth is that God is pursuing you, whether you know it or not. Even if you are intentionally running in the opposite direction, he is pursuing you. The moment you slow down and stop running, God will be right there, calmly walking toward you. Despite what you may think, there is nothing you can do that could separate you from the love of God. There is no mistake too big, no mistake done too often, that can make it too late.

Recovery is possible.

It was possible for me.

It is possible for you.

afterword

In the Crucible

—— *Rob* ——

While our story has what most would call a "happy ending," I don't want to ignore the needs and pain of families for whom no end to the addiction is in sight. Where the addict shows no sign of repentance or desire to change. Where rehab and recovery seem like an impossible dream. Where the relational, financial, spiritual, and emotional devastation are ongoing—and increasing.

Many of the principles we laid out in this book still hold, even when you don't see any positive progress in your loved one. You still need to rely on God's strength and the support of his body, the church. You still need to live one day at a time, trusting in God's goodness and provision and serving those around you. And you still need to make sure you are not enabling your loved one but are allowing them to experience the consequences of their own actions.

Families and friends of addicts should seek out counseling if possible. In addition, they should consider joining support groups such as Al-Anon, which expressly offer help to families and friends of alcoholics. Celebrate Recovery can also be helpful to families and friends of addicts by educating them about addiction and supporting them as they deal with the issues and the pain of a loved one's addiction.

While we deeply believe that recovery is possible for anyone, we don't want to be naive and declare that it is likely for everyone. Our world is tragically broken, and we and all of creation groan as we wait for our Savior's healing touch. But we are not alone. In the worst of times, we need to hold firmly to the glorious words of the apostle Paul:

> I consider that our present sufferings are not worth comparing with the glory that will be revealed in us. For the creation waits in eager expectation for the children of God to be revealed. For the creation was subjected to frustration, not by its own choice, but by the will of the one who subjected it, in hope that the creation itself will be liberated from its bondage to decay and brought into the freedom and glory of the children of God.
>
> We know that the whole creation has been groaning as in the pains of childbirth right up to the present time. Not only so, but we ourselves, who have the firstfruits of the Spirit, groan inwardly as we wait eagerly for our adoption to sonship, the redemption of our bodies. For in this hope we were saved. But hope that is seen is no hope at all.

Who hopes for what they already have? But if we hope for what we do not yet have, we wait for it patiently.

In the same way, the Spirit helps us in our weakness. We do not know what we ought to pray for, but the Spirit himself intercedes for us through wordless groans . . .

And we know that in all things God works for the good of those who love him, who have been called according to his purpose.

Romans 8:18–26, 28

Acknowledgments

To our families and friends—we love doing life together with you. Your encouragement and prayerful support mean the world to us.

To the Shoreline Church staff—we simply love serving Jesus alongside each of you. Your enthusiasm is contagious, and your creativity and hard work inspire us.

To Shoreline Church—you're the best congregation on the planet!

To our Zondervan family: vice president of marketing Tom Dean, executive editor Carolyn McCready, and senior editor Dirk Buursma—we never expected to receive such personal warmth and encouragement in the process of writing this book. Thank you so much for your wisdom and help in shaping this project. It means the world to us that you believe in our story.

To The Fedd Agency—thank you, Esther, for getting this process started. And thank you, Whitney Gossett, for guiding us every step along the way

To our writing coaches: A. J. Gregory—you wrote the first chapter with us; Kendall Davis—you coached us through every chapter and page. Thank you both for investing your incredible skills in us.

To the Arbor—thank you for taking Danielle in and starting her on her road to freedom.

To AA and Celebrate Recovery—you are the true heroes of the recovery movement. We along with millions of others have benefited from your care and dedication.

To all recovering addicts, to those who have paved the way before us—thank you for showing us the way. To those who come after us, we are honored to add our story to your journey.

To our Lord and Savior, Jesus Christ—you did for us what we could never do for ourselves. Thank you for your grace, which has forgiven us and made us brand-new. We stand in you alone. And thank you for letting us steal your most famous story and change the name to "Prodigal Daughter."